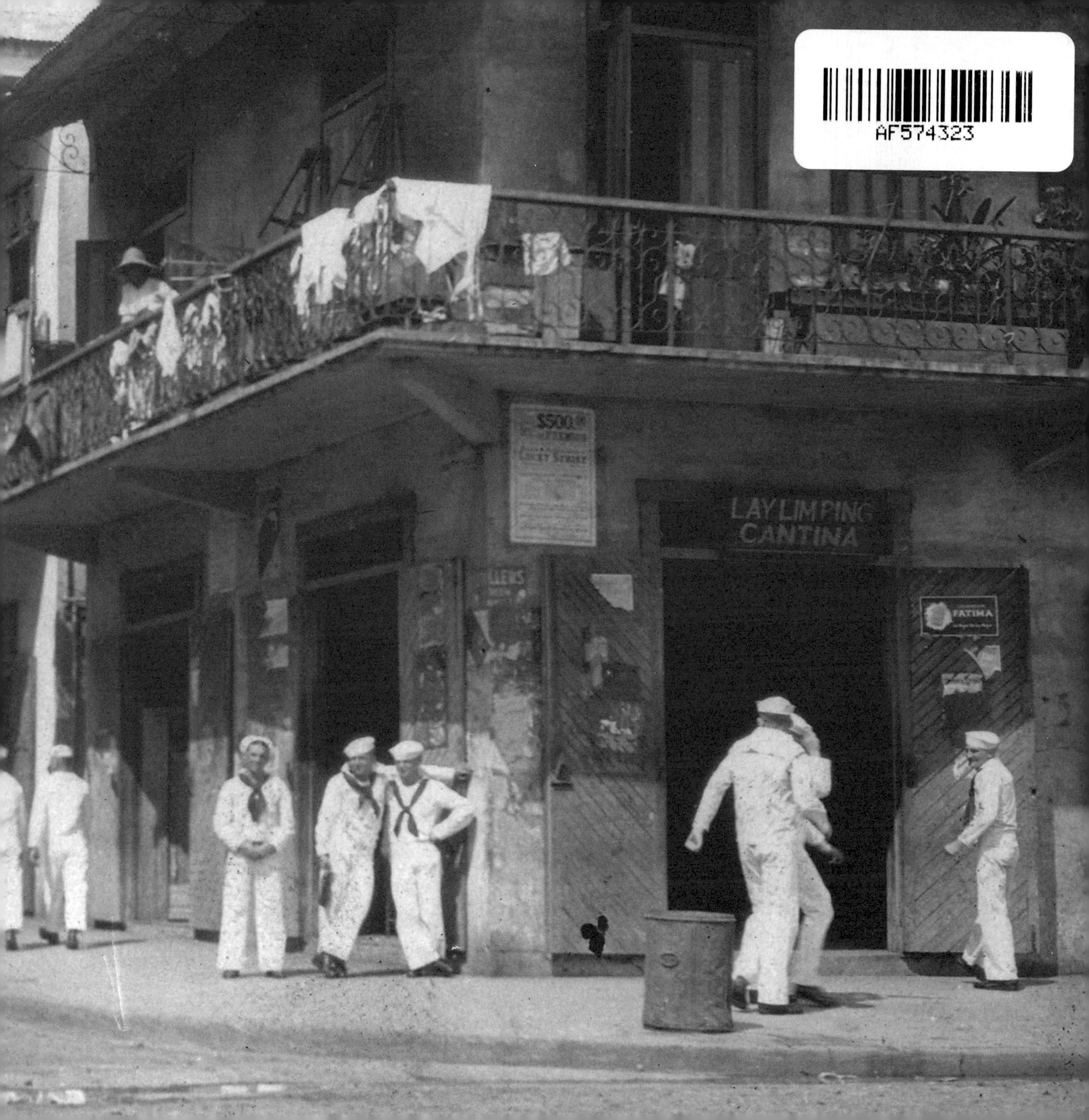
LAY LIM PING
CANTINA
FATIMA

SAILOR

VINTAGE PHOTOS
OF A
MASCULINE ICON

Edited and with an Introduction by

Kevin Bentley

Council Oak Books
San Francisco / Tulsa

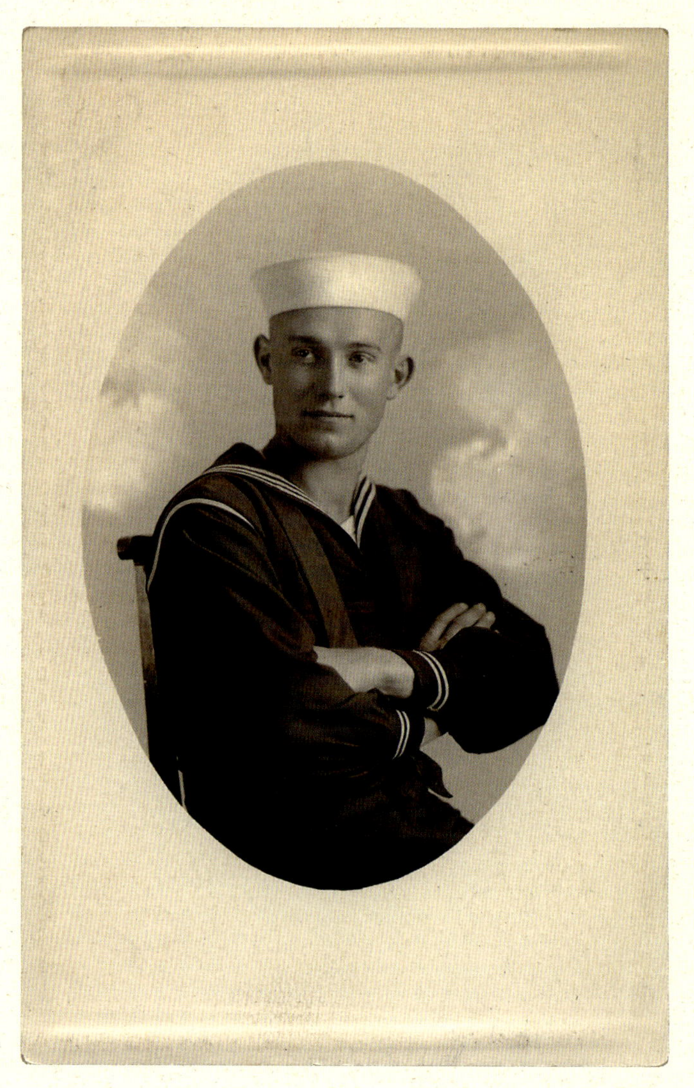

Introduction

I've always been drawn to old photographs of people. I was the family photo archivist as a child, organizing and repairing the fat maroon album that began with my parents' honeymoon, swelled with pictures of my older brother's infancy and petered out during mine. Most of all I loved the little tan Brownie snapshot album my mother had kept as a child, neatly pasted with tall, deco-bordered 30s snaps of herself and her sister, two little girls with dark Buster Brown hairdos, tap shoes, and a violin and an accordion respectively. I marveled that this little tap dancing violinist could have turned into my no-nonsense mom. History stopped there; my father had no family photographs, and my maternal grandparents had both come from poor East Texas farmers whose fore-bears probably never had a camera. My grandfather's bottom dresser drawer held, amid old hunting magazines and pungent Prince Albert cans, a couple of worn, turn-of-the-century group portraits of unidentified, scowling country people. Once, though, during a hot, dreamy Sunday afternoon snooping session, I discovered a large yellowed envelope at the bottom of his sock drawer. I pulled out a handful of 20s-era snapshots of a short, flirtatious-looking girl—not my grandmother—posing alongside a farmhouse, cotton fields, and a Model T (*Darling, of you I am dreaming* had been penned across the bottom border of one). Then, deeper down: a full-length studio portrait mounted on stiff board of a bareheaded sailor posing with one hand on a fancy chair. On the back, penciled in a childish scrawl: *Uncle Taylor Lowrie. Died Hong Kong 1912*. He looked very young, very handsome, and exotically far from my humdrum suburban Texas town.

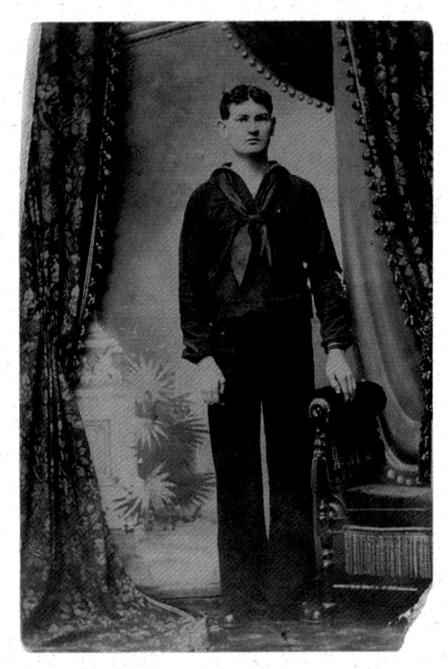

That, I suppose, is where this book began. Or here: pacing the aisles of a large antique show a couple of years ago, I came upon a little six-by-ten-inch soft leather photo album with a cut-out silk silhouette of a battleship mounted on the front, a nineteen-year-old sailor's snapshot record of his first voyage—to Hawaii, Pago Pago and Australia—in 1925. Bound into the front was a daily ship's log, which, like most youthful diaries, had been left blank after about a dozen sporadic entries. There was an odd diploma, an elaborate certificate from The Domain of Neptunus Rex, confirming the sailor's initiation into the Solemn Mysteries of the Ancient Order of the Deep. Tucked into the back was a spartan Christmas dinner menu with a moldering red tassel. In-between were page after page of beautiful black and white snapshots of the sailor and his mates at sea—swimming in a pool made from stretched tarps, running laps around the deck, hanging laundry over the railings—and roaming the streets in port.

I'd been casually sifting through old individual photos and postcards at fairs and junk shops for years, buying what caught my eye and my imagination. Now I began to come across photos of sailors more often, or maybe I just began to notice them with more interest. I found a couple of other complete albums, one small and thick, packed with one-and-one-half-inch high photos of a 1918 sailor and his pals. But it's still the single, completely anonymous images pulled from a shoebox on a dusty shelf that affect me most, artifacts of some planet—a life—blown apart decades ago and drifted to earth. I bought a new acid-free snapshot album with a laminated sailor photo on the front, and began arranging my loose finds in it with old corner mounts, poring over them like a boy with a stamp collection, while my partner peered at me over his newspaper and shook his head. "You sure have some imagination," he said.

The photographs of sailors reproduced in this book are drawn from those I've amassed and from another private collection. Discovered at auctions, antique and junk shops, and flea markets, through death or life's vagaries, they've endured. Like all vernacular photography they are poignant in their anonymity. We stare back at the direct gaze of these young men and wonder what they were thinking at the exact moment the shutter opened, what happened next, where the rest of their lives took them. The earnest studio portraits are as familiar as our relatives' bureau tops, or the cedar chest-stored family album. They preserve an idealized self meant for sending home, for posterity.

The snapshots chronicle good times—no journalistic battle scenes here. The only hint of that lies in the caught-off-guard expressions on some of these men's faces, or the mostly playful poses with the ship's guns. Otherwise, these photos ignore the tedium and danger of war.

As much as the cowboy or flying ace, the sailor is an instantly recognizable character in our imaginations. Cast large from Ishmael to Gene Kelly and Frank Sinatra in *On the Town* and *Anchors Aweigh*, from Genet's *Querelle* to the logo on the Players cigarette pack, the sailor is an emblem of virile masculinity, adventure and romantic opportunity. He might be pining for the girl he left behind, or bragging of conquests in exotic ports-of-call like Hong Kong, Panama City or San Juan, but we imagine him lonely and seeking companionship: the words "Fleet's In!" have all the fruitful connotations of an ancient fertility rite. A boy in a sailor uniform is a byword for fresh-faced youth and inexperience, optimistic and adventurous, up against the wiles of old salts and sophisticated cities. He has "the good looks, cheery health, and frank enjoyment of young life" personified by Melville's *Billy Budd*. Unlike more rigid military figures, sailors are limber, and in these photos they lean, bend and curve like gymnasts, at ease, and easy in their physical proximity to each other, embodying their freewheeling, live-and-let-live reputation.

What do you do with a drunken sailor? An inebriated sailor might be "rolled" or "Shanghaid." My own great uncle Taylor Lowrie (page two), whose photo I unearthed from my grandfather's sock drawer, was thrown from a second floor window in a Hong Kong barroom brawl in 1912 and sent back to Beckville, Texas in a sealed metal casket. Suspicious relatives pried it open to confirm his identity, and my then eight-year-old grandfather, hoisted up for a look, recognized the curly black hair of the admired uncle who'd sent him postcards from around the world. I chose that photo when my grandfather died, and it's been a kind of talisman to me since, evoking youthful glamour and adventure—and its risks.

Sailors are frank; they don't mince words. They swear like—sailors. Many of their nicknames and superstitions are firmly lodged in the nineteenth century: sea gypsy, swabbie, gob, deck ape, tar. *Red sky at night, sailor's delight; red sky at morning, sailor take warning.* Any number of water-spilling mishaps might also presage a doomed voyage; patting a woman intimately was said to assure a safe passage, though this tradition seems suspect. Touching a sailor's collar before he set sail was said to bring good luck. As with other denizens of traditionally all-male societies, sailors' lingo has always been bawdy: *boy butter* (the grease used on torpedoes); *Sea Daddy* (one who takes an inexperienced crewmate under his wing). As with other fraternities, there were rites of initiation: the line-crossing ceremony or "jumping the line" hazing ritual performed at a sailor's first crossing of the equator. Novices, or "Pollywogs," were made to endure disgusting ordeals in full view of King Neptune and his court; afterward they could bask in the ranks of "Shellbacks."

It's easy to romanticize the job you don't have. I grew up an army brat, surrounded by GI's in bulky fatigues. There was little likelihood of my entering the military; I tried ROTC for a few weeks in high school to evade PE, and got drummed out because I couldn't tell left from right. But it seemed to me as a boy that when older men referred to a hitch in the navy, they did so with a fond, wistful tone. With the army, you got drafted; the marines were about proving one's toughness—but the air force and navy seemed to have more to do with a specific passion—for flying, or going to sea. We think of young men who were a little too adventurous, who may have gotten into minor trouble, or who needed to escape small town or family constraints running off to join the navy. As one who fled a backwater hometown at twenty-one, I'm interested in departures, voyages out. The wet-behind-the-ears boy ships out to see the world, and comes back changed: tanned, muscular, cigar-smoking, stamped with tattoos—masculine, worldly. What happens out there in that secret, enclosed world of a ship at sea?

For someone shy, self-conscious and private, it's both scary and fascinating to imagine these sailors sequestered on a few hundred feet of steel in the middle of a vast, beautiful, dangerous sea. Living in such close quarters, these men must have forged friendships that went far beyond the bounds of later 50s-era competition, suspicion and conformity. In photo after photo of sailors with their arms draped over each other's shoulders, we witness this unself-conscious physical intimacy. Maybe because my father had no friends to speak of, and because I was for a time a schoolyard misfit, I envy the male camaraderie I see in these sailor pictures.

Appealing, touching and enigmatic in all their variety—daguerreotype, tintype, cabinet card, *carte-de-visite*, RealPhoto postcard, photo-booth strip, studio portrait and snapshot—the photographs in this book show us the individual faces of a larger-than-life figure, from the adolescent purity of Charlie Olsen of Livermore on page eleven to the knowing gaze of the mugshot on page eighty-two. Some of the snapshots show sailors back home on leave posing with girlfriend, sister, or the family dog, a comfortable old house in the background. Has the sailor sitting on the front steps on page ninety-three just returned home after a long absence? Or is someone holding him back for one last bittersweet remembrance before he ships out again? In some cases a photo's deep wear indicates it was likely carried for years in wallet or pocketbook, held dear.

In twenty-three years of living in the port city of San Francisco, I've seen my own aging reflected back at me as I've distantly observed the periodic waves of white- or navy-clad sailors spilling over North Beach and across town, heralded by the thunderclap of the Blue Angels. They've changed before my eyes from charismatic, boisterous contemporaries to shockingly young, eager (boisterous) adolescents. My regard feels avuncular, sentimental. Even as I admire their good looks and daydream of their adventures, I have some of that same feeling for the subjects of these photos. ⚓

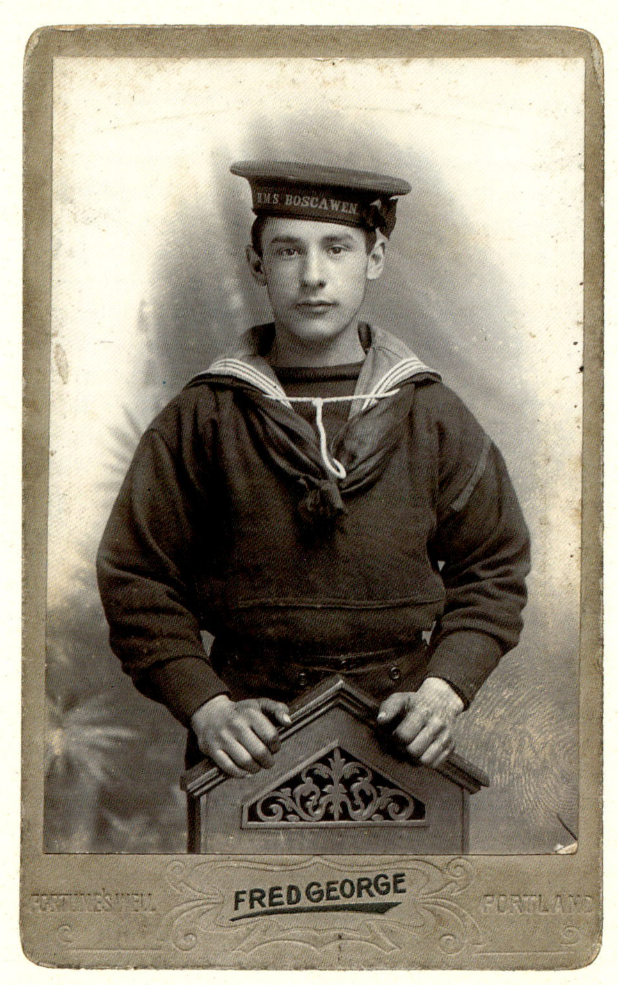
H.M.S. BOSCAWEN
FRED GEORGE
FORTUNE'S WELL
PORTLAND

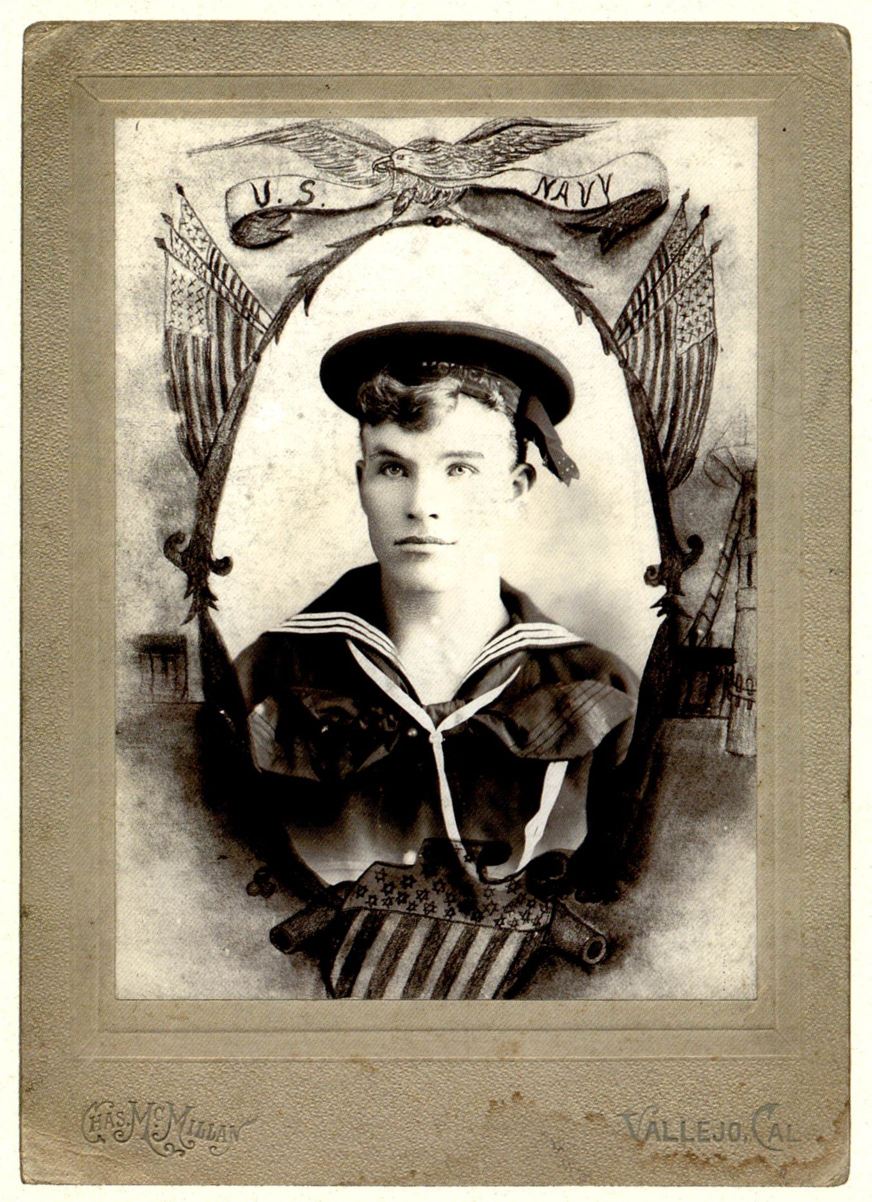
U.S. NAVY
CHAS. McMILLAN
VALLEJO, CAL.

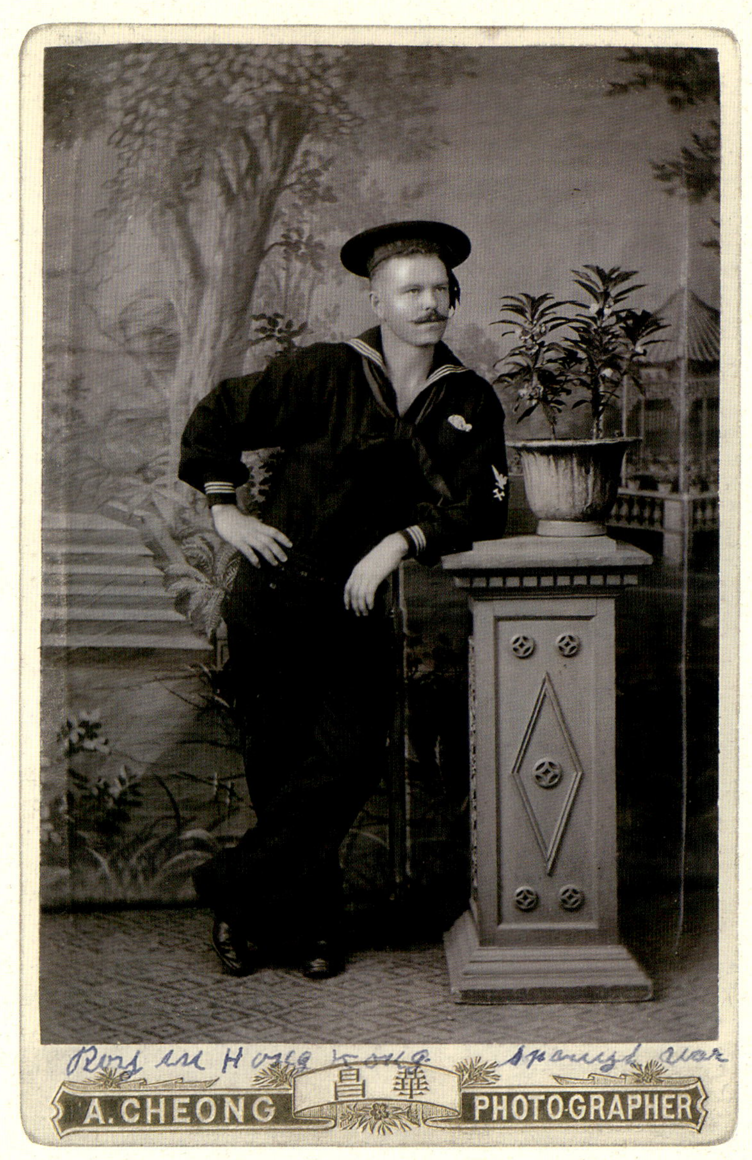
Boy in Hong Kong Spanish war
A. CHEONG
昌華
PHOTOGRAPHER

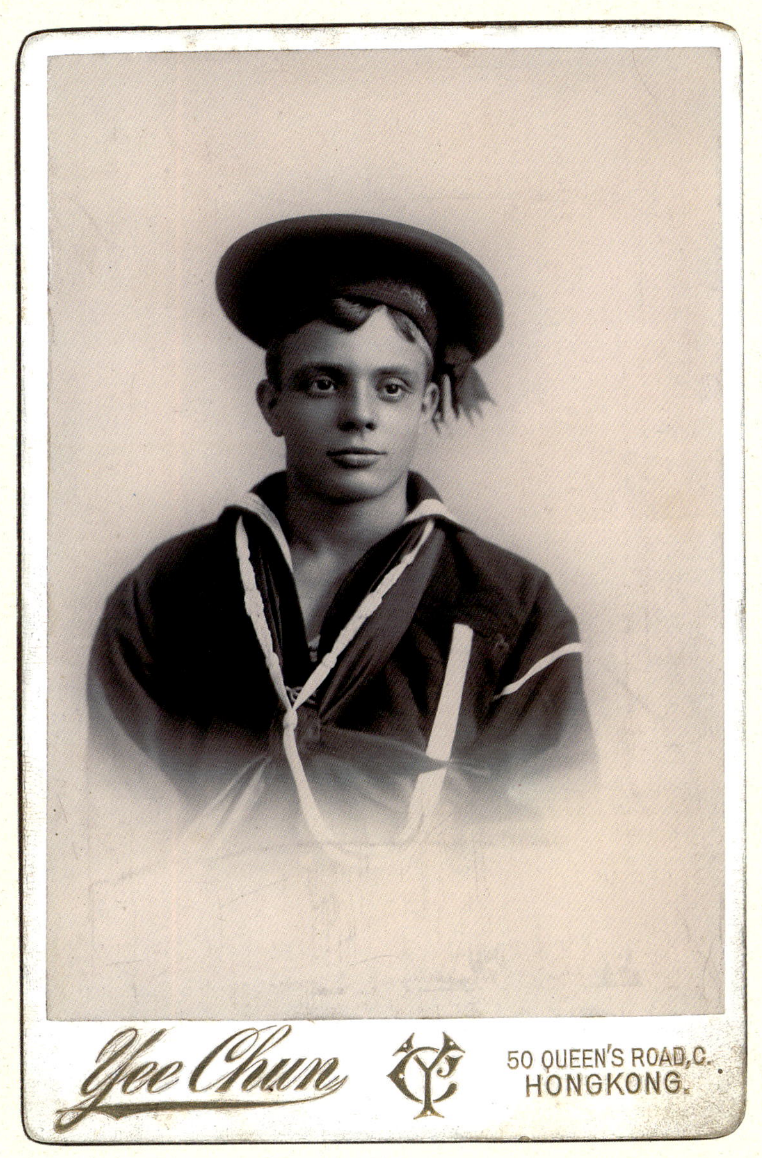
Yee Chun
YC
50 QUEEN'S ROAD, C.
HONGKONG.

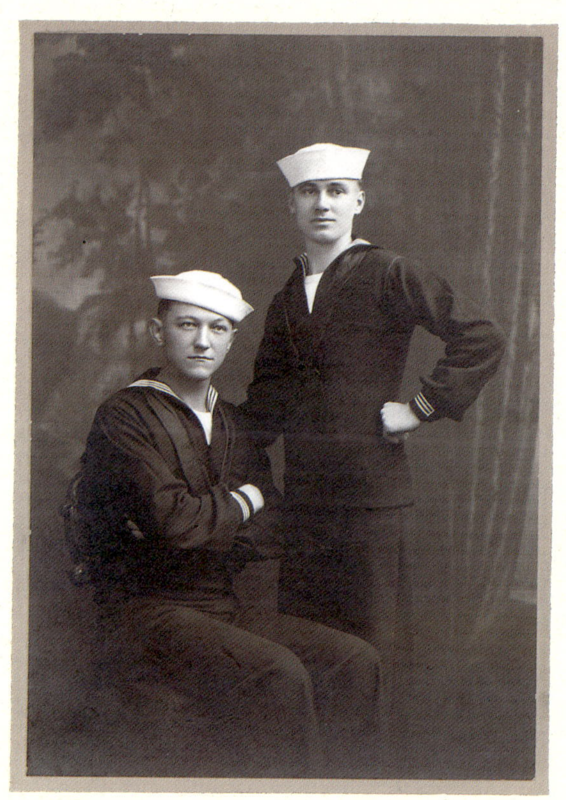

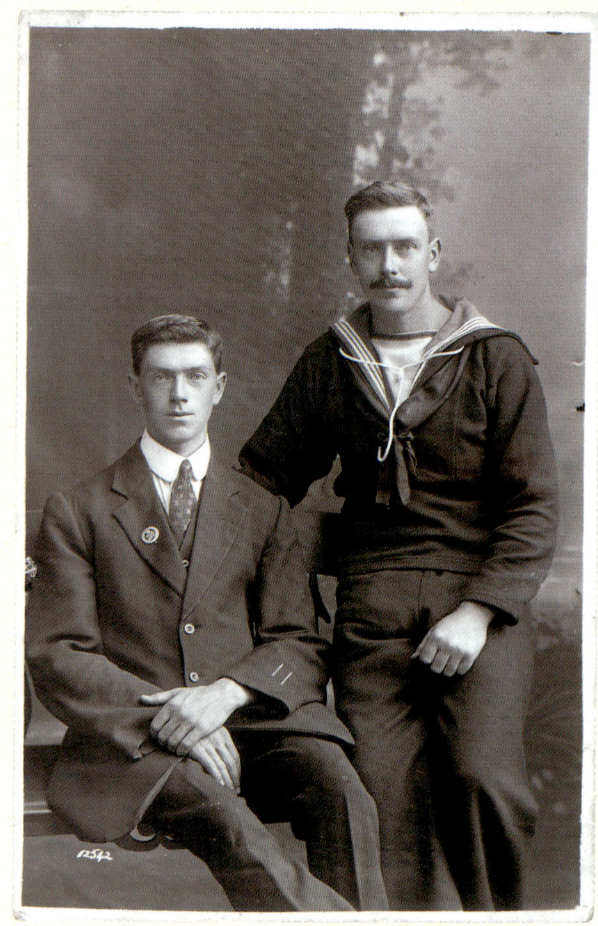

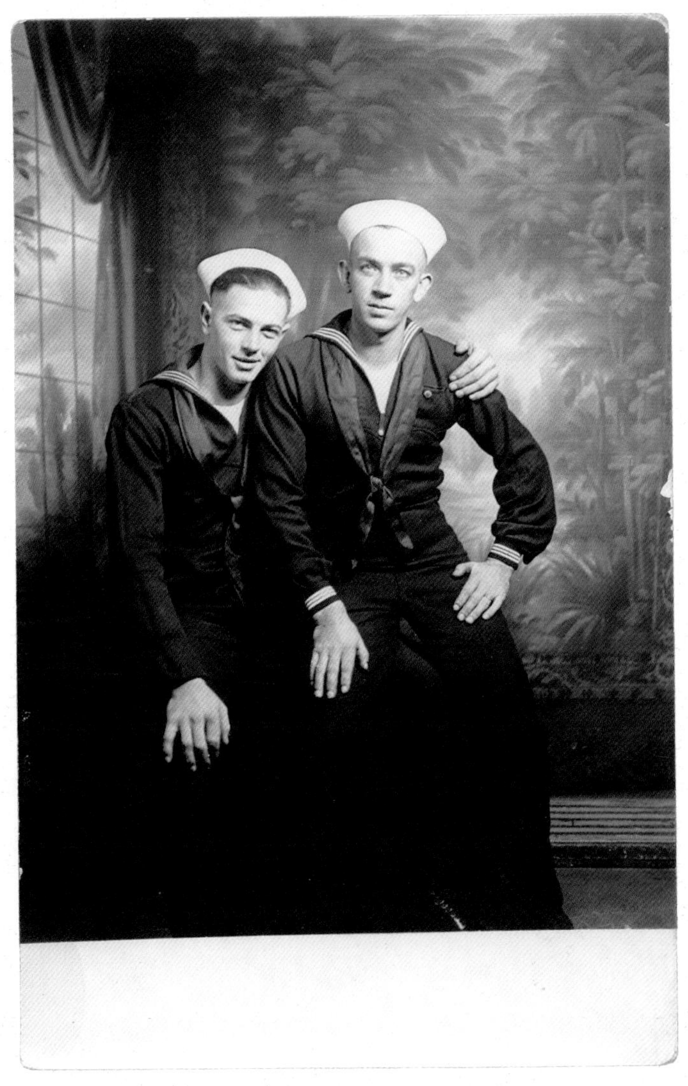

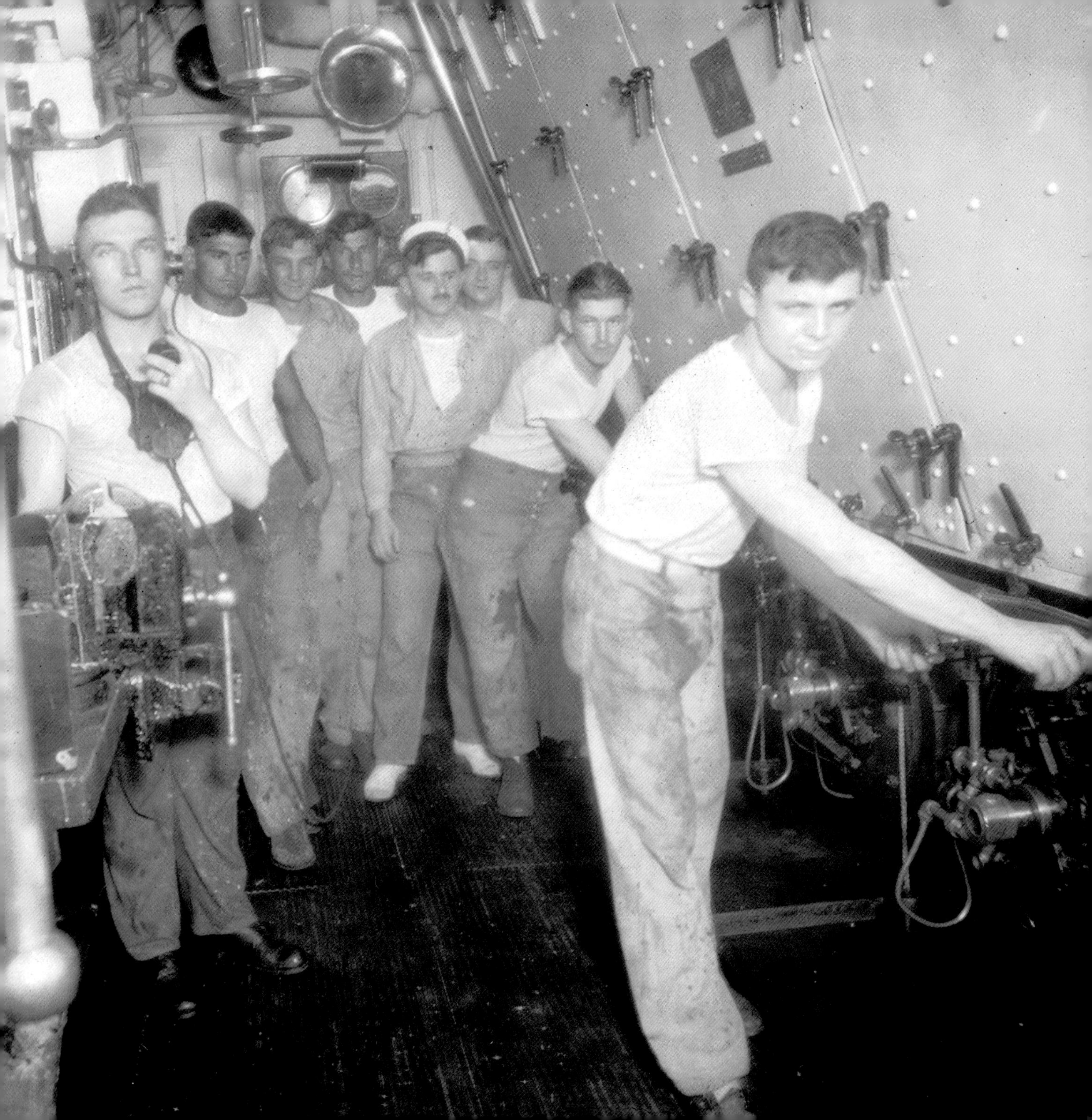

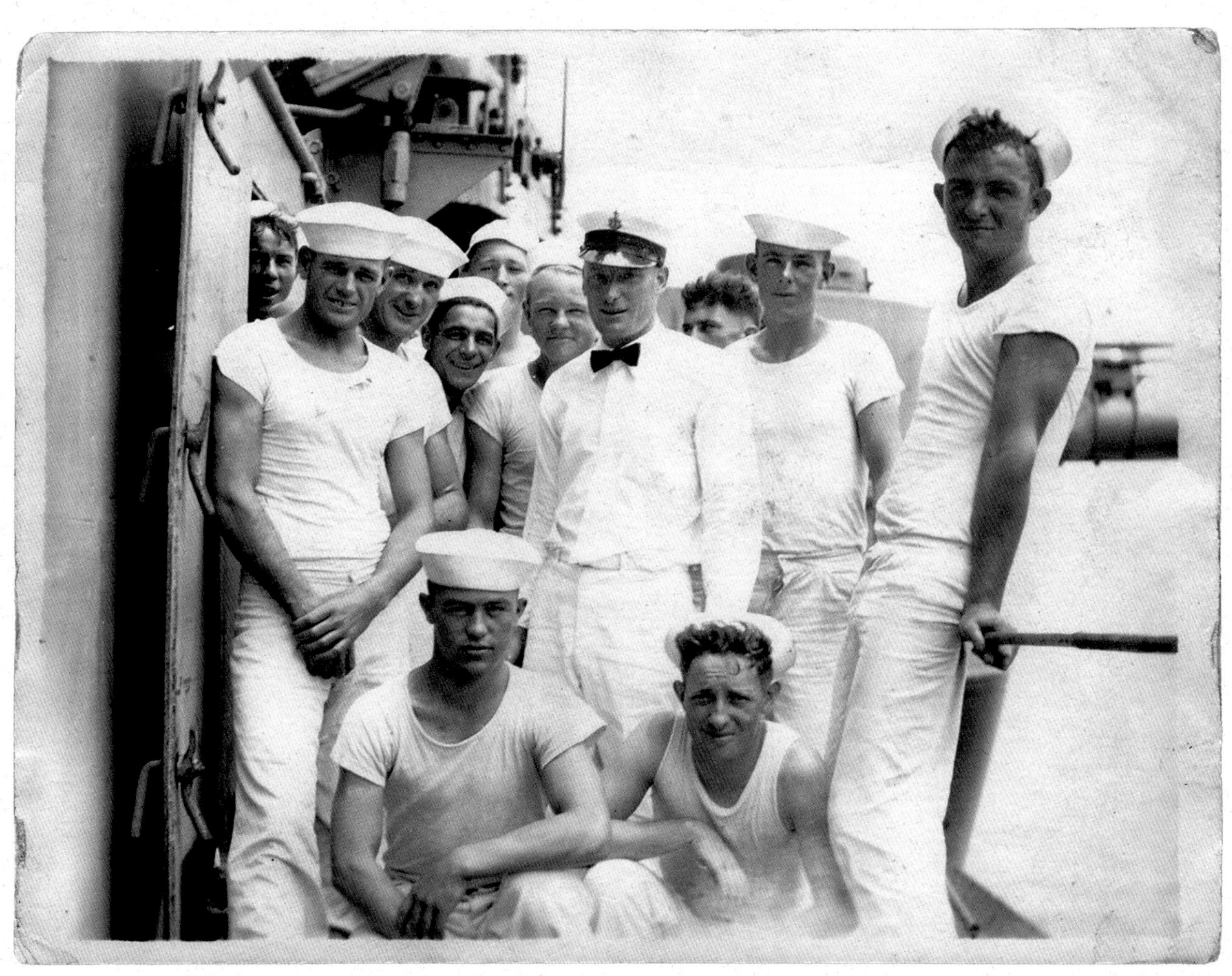

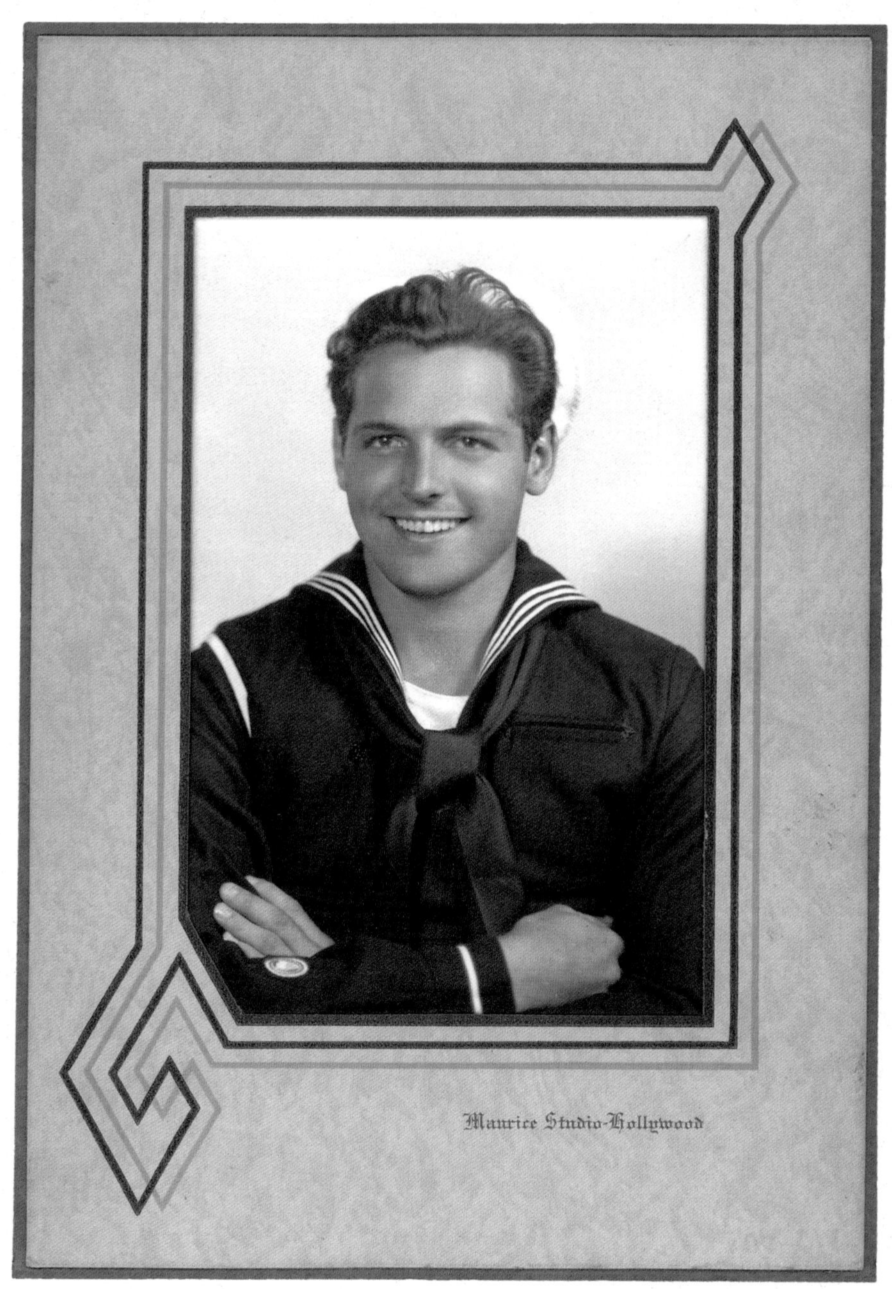
Maurice Studio-Hollywood

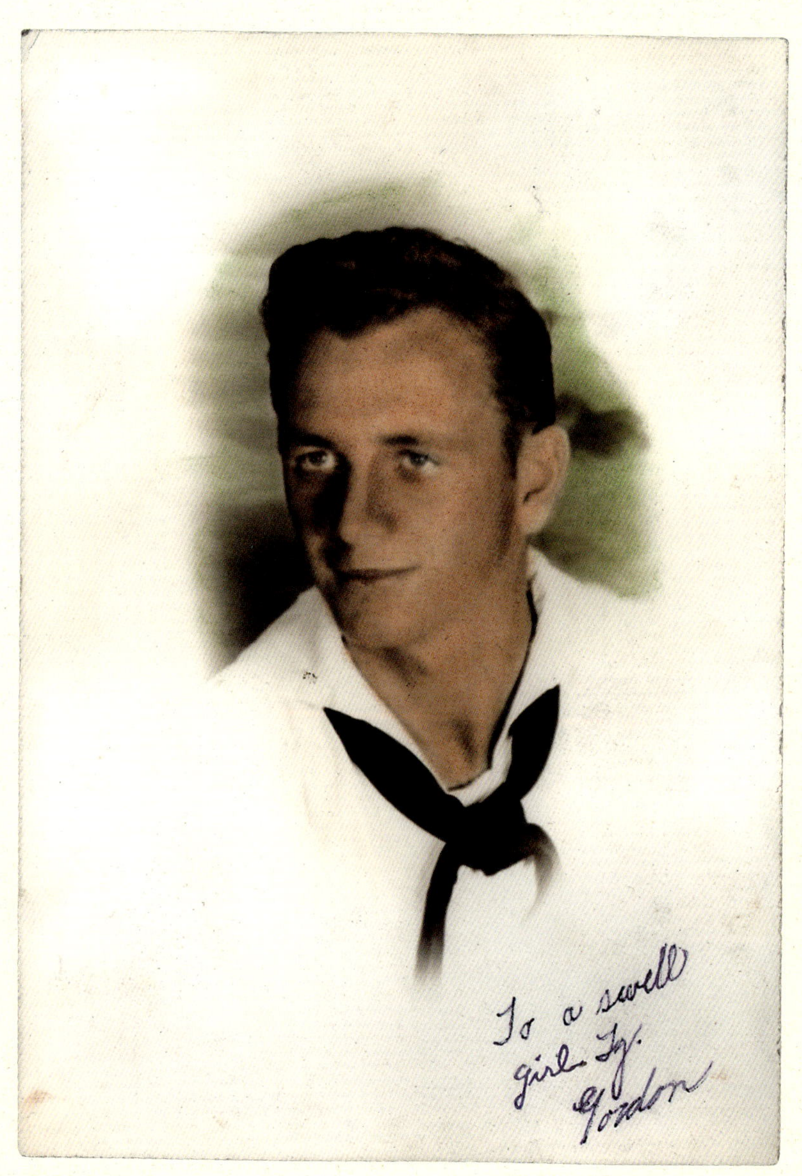
To a swell
girl. Ty.
Gordon

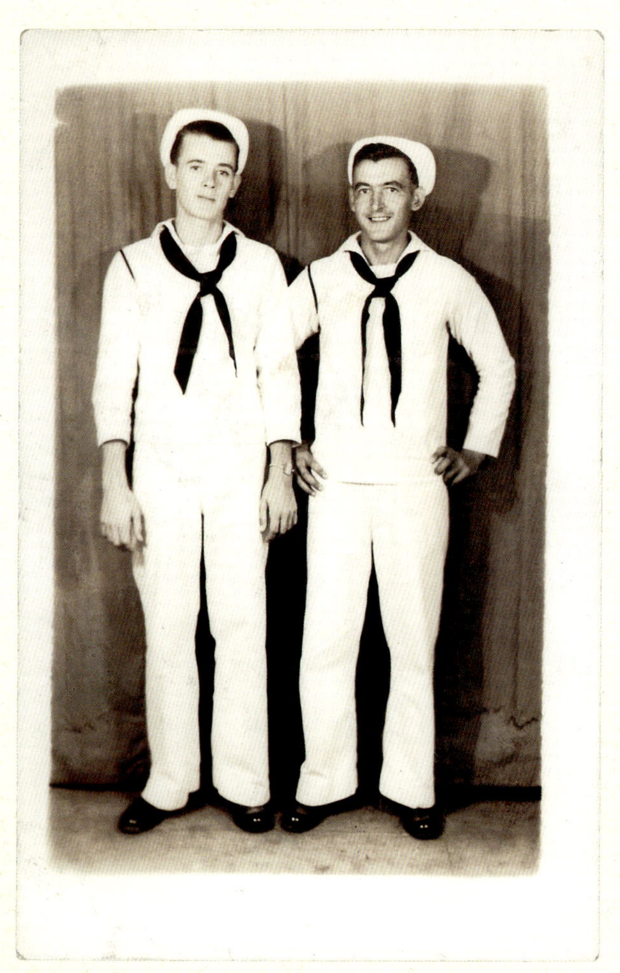

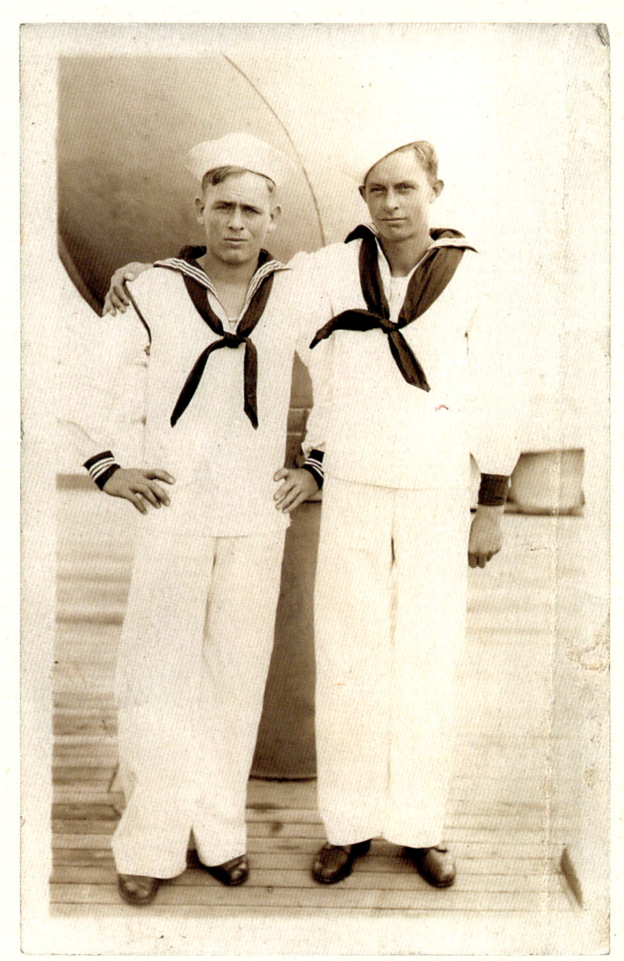

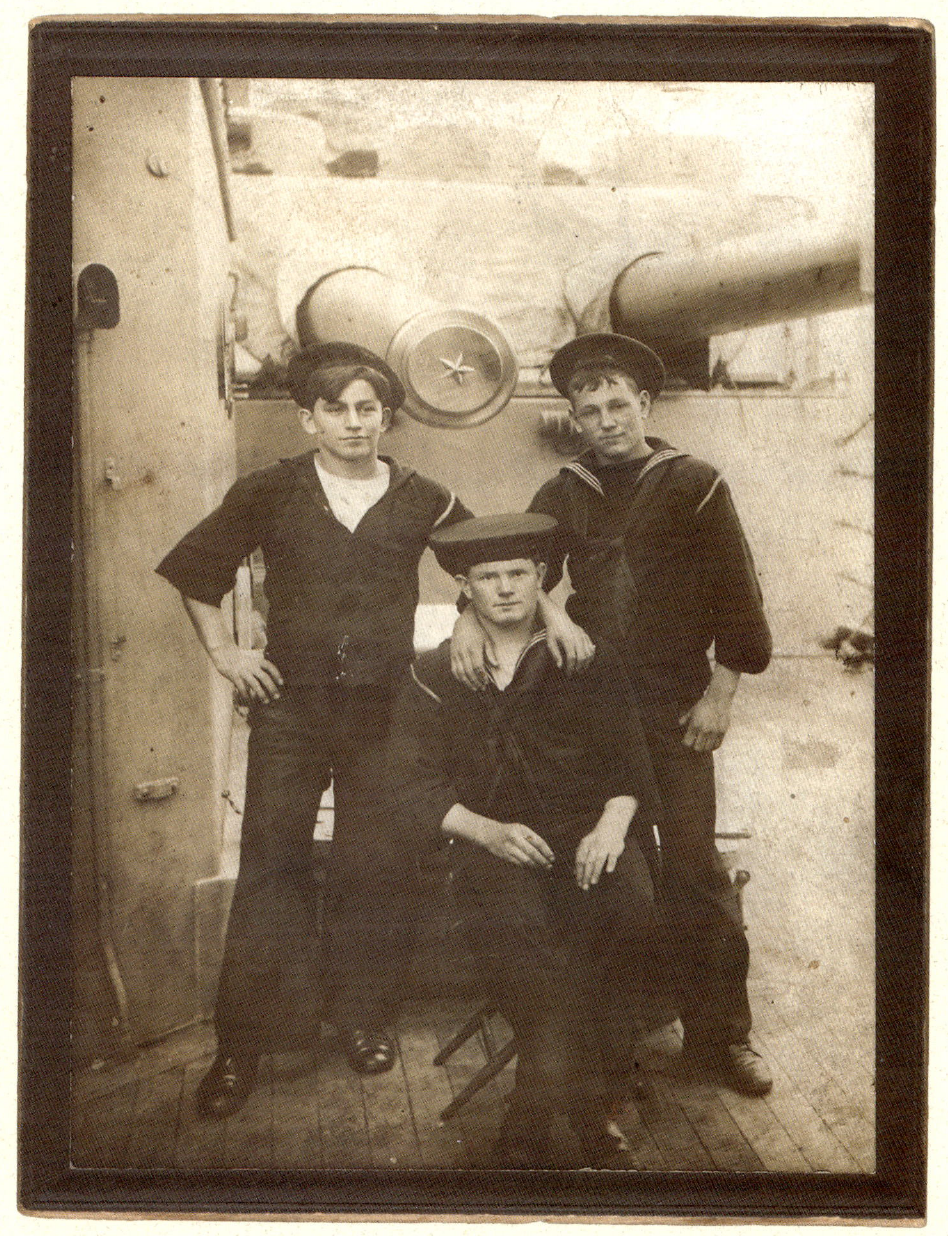

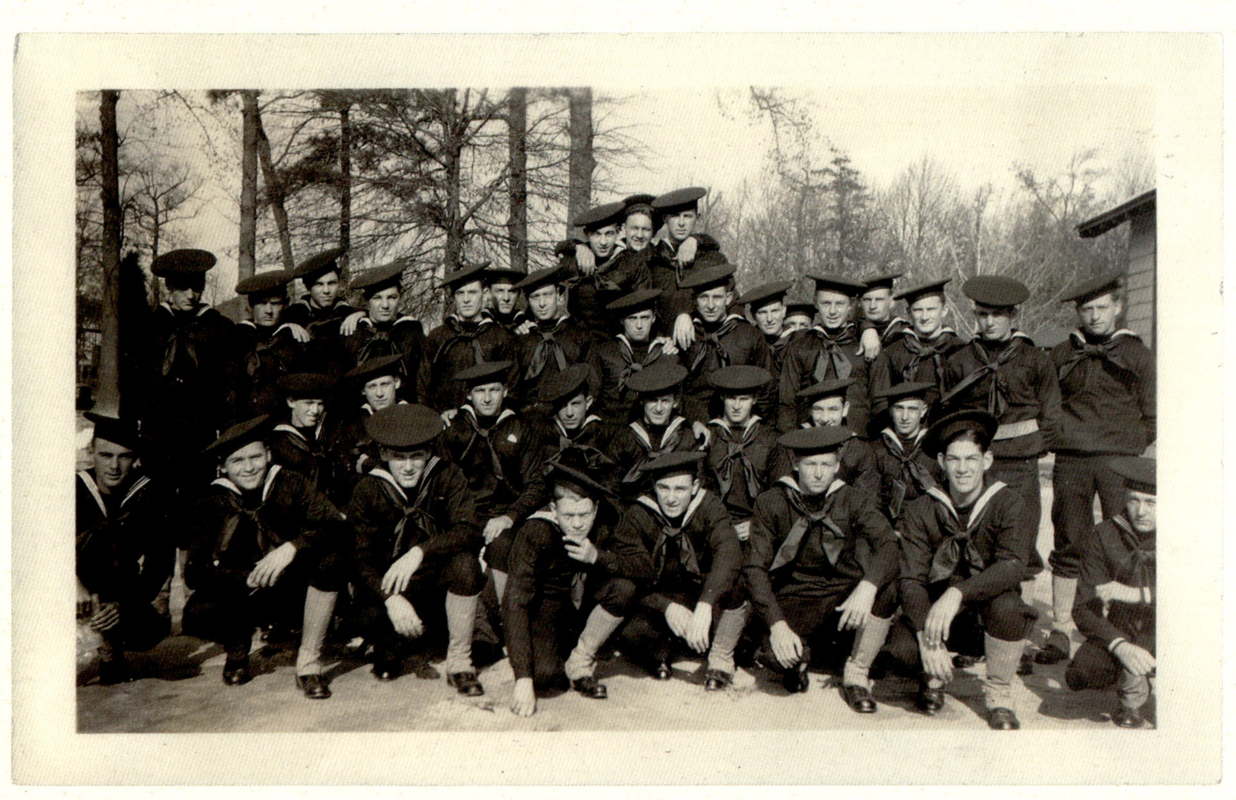

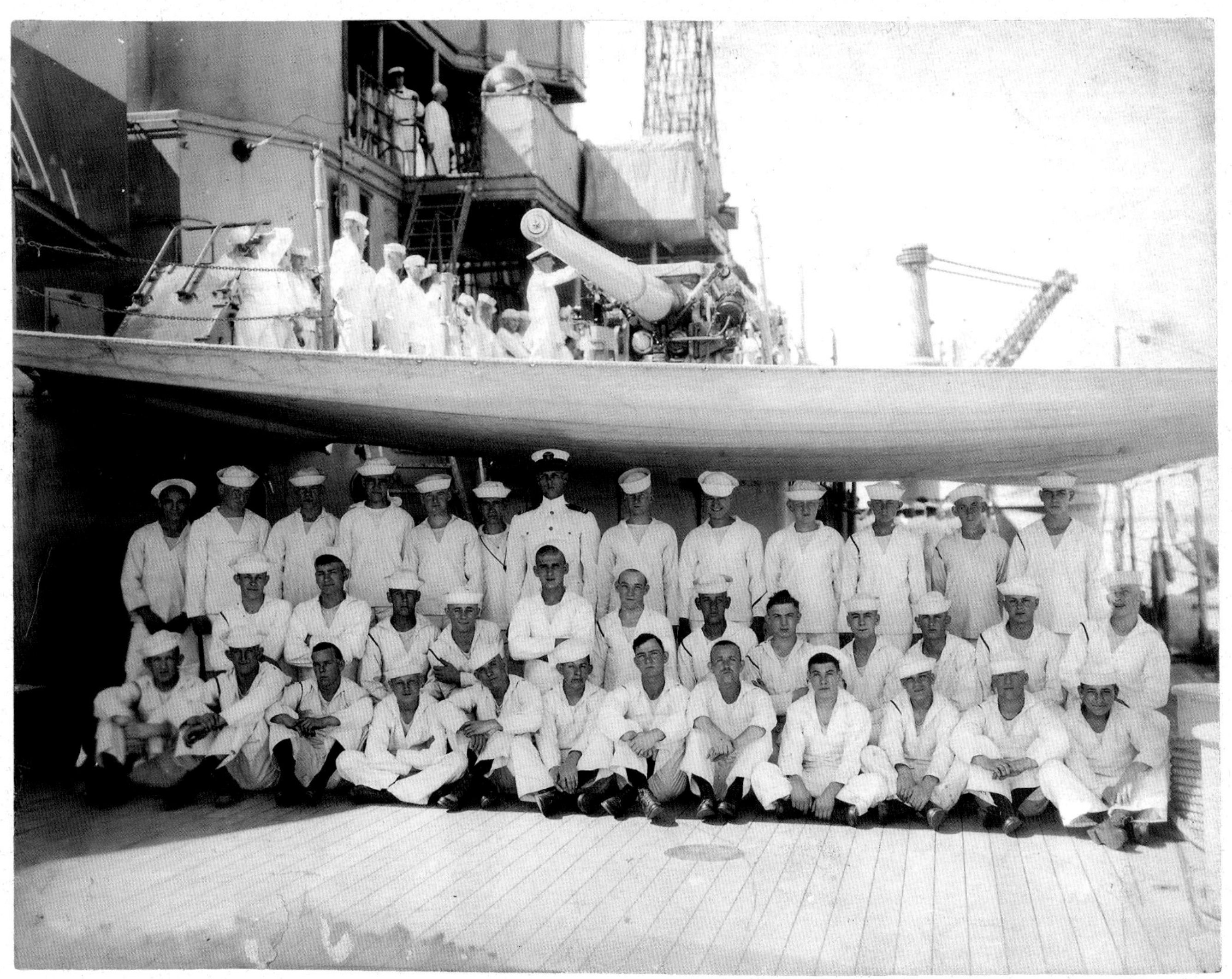

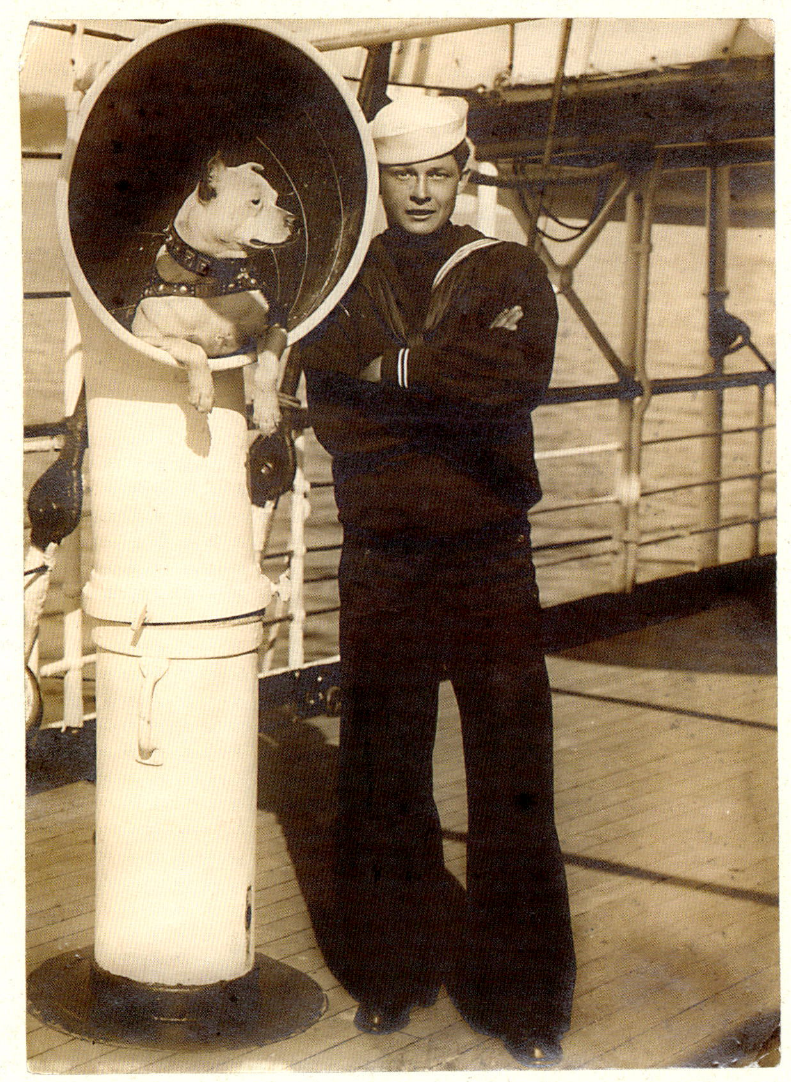

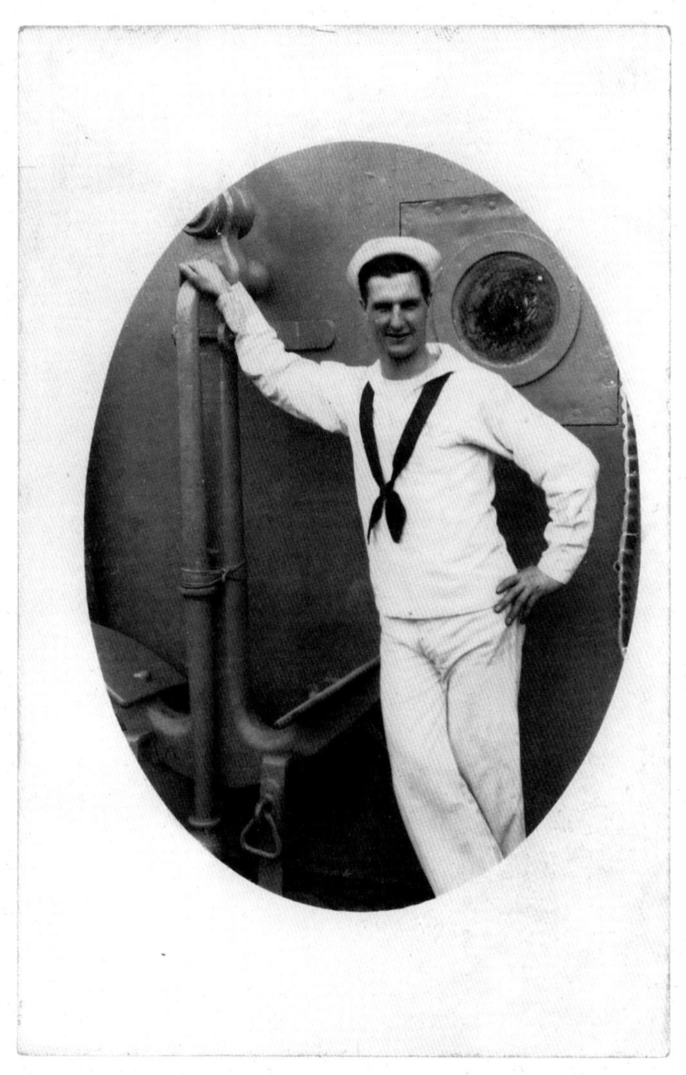

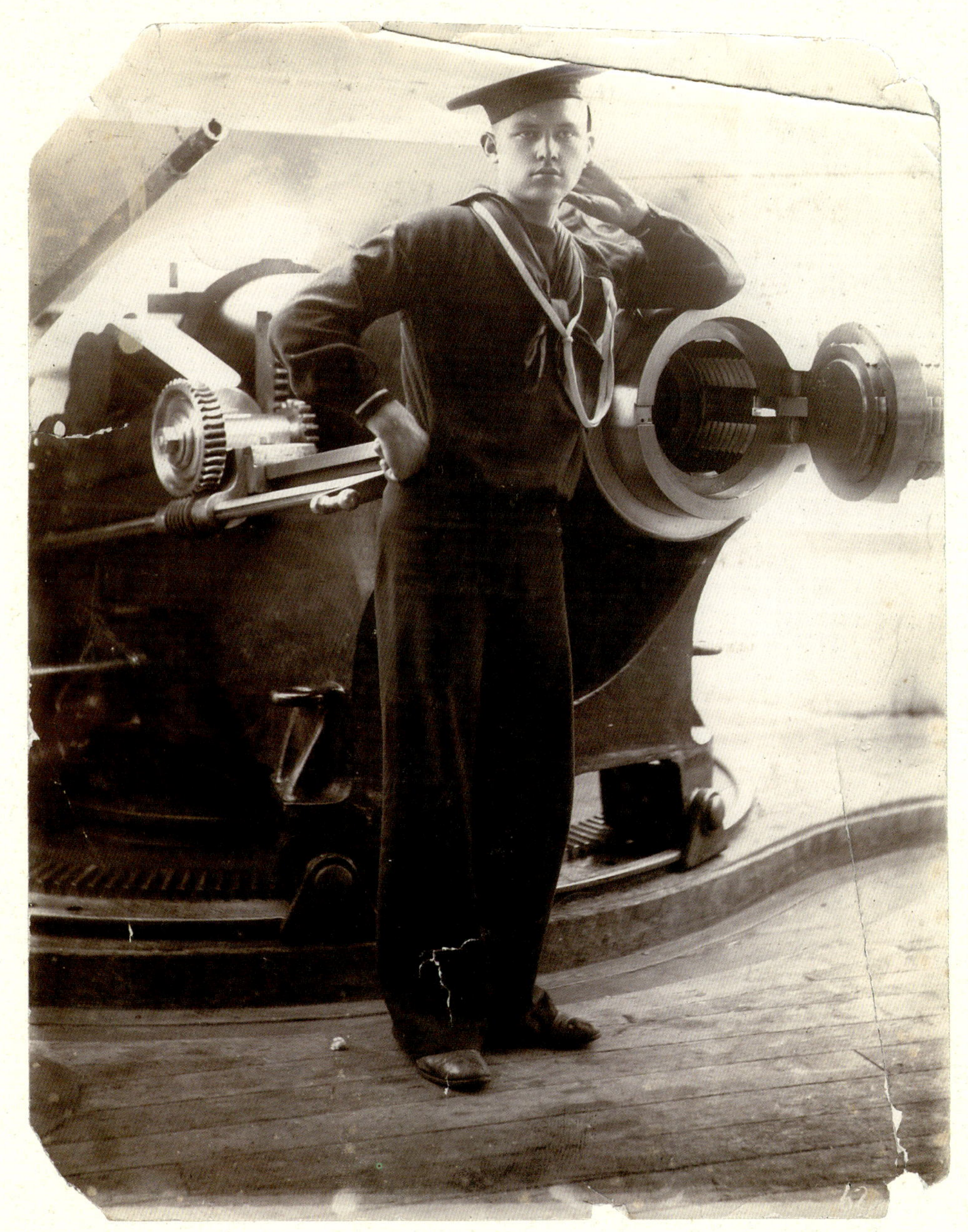

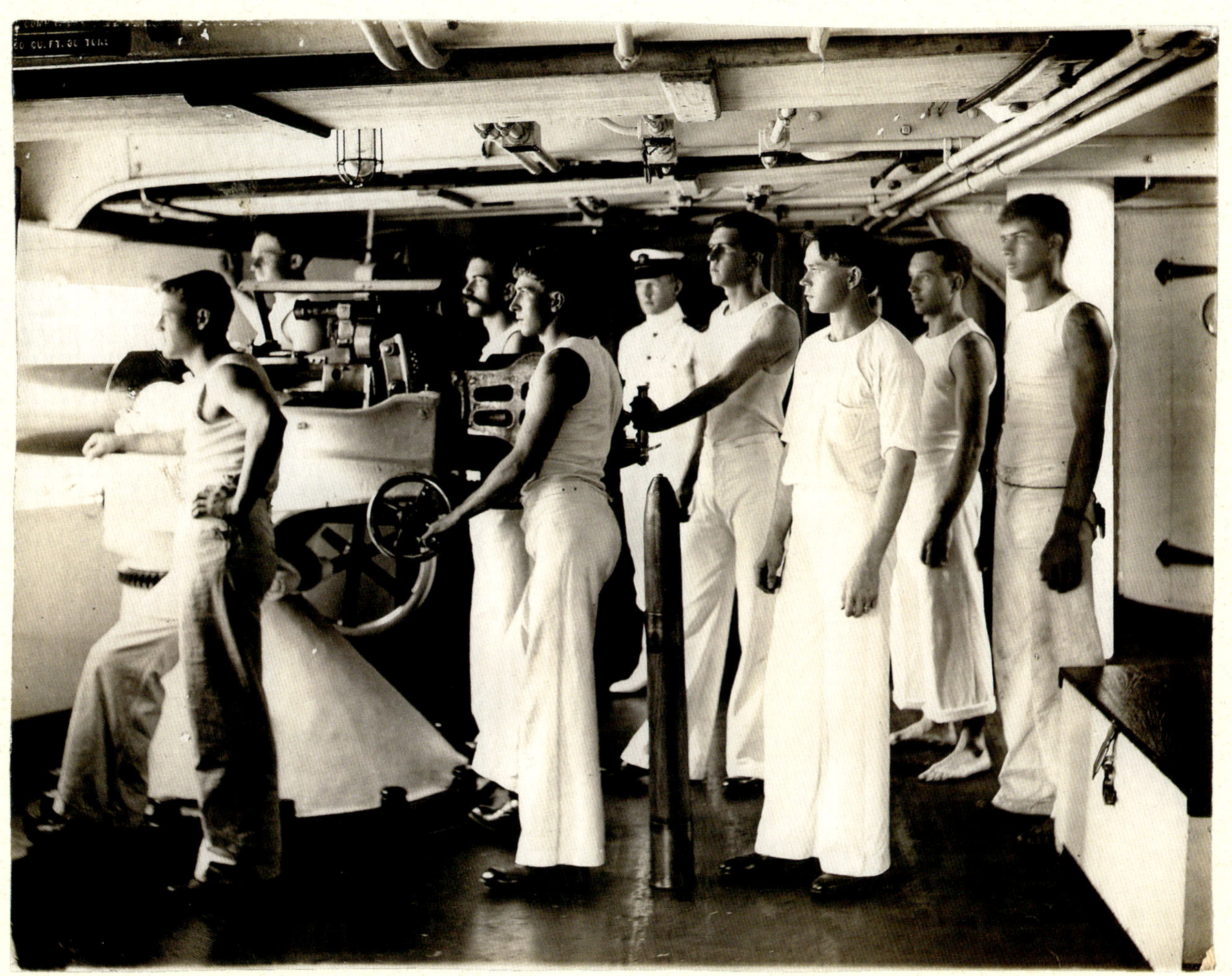

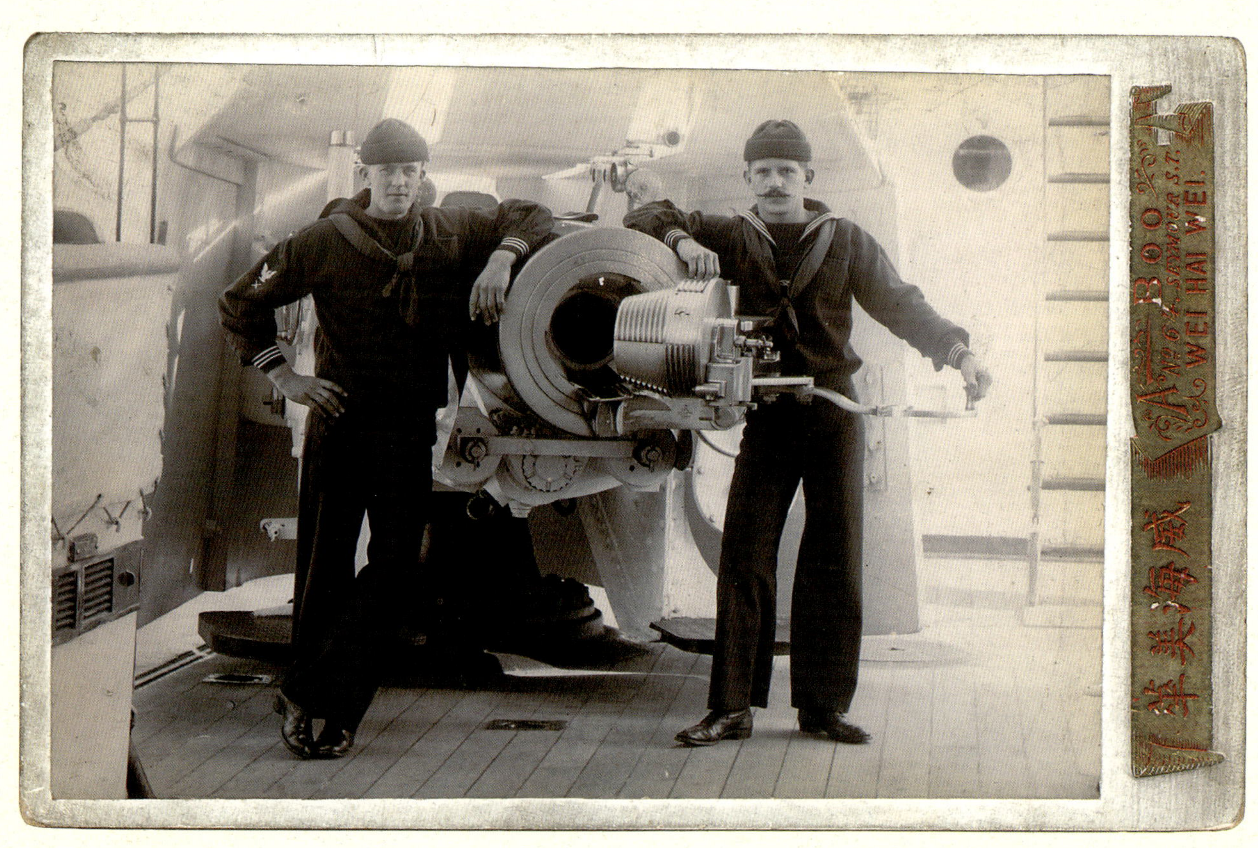
A BOO
No 64 SEYMOUR ST.
WEI HAI WEI.
威海美華

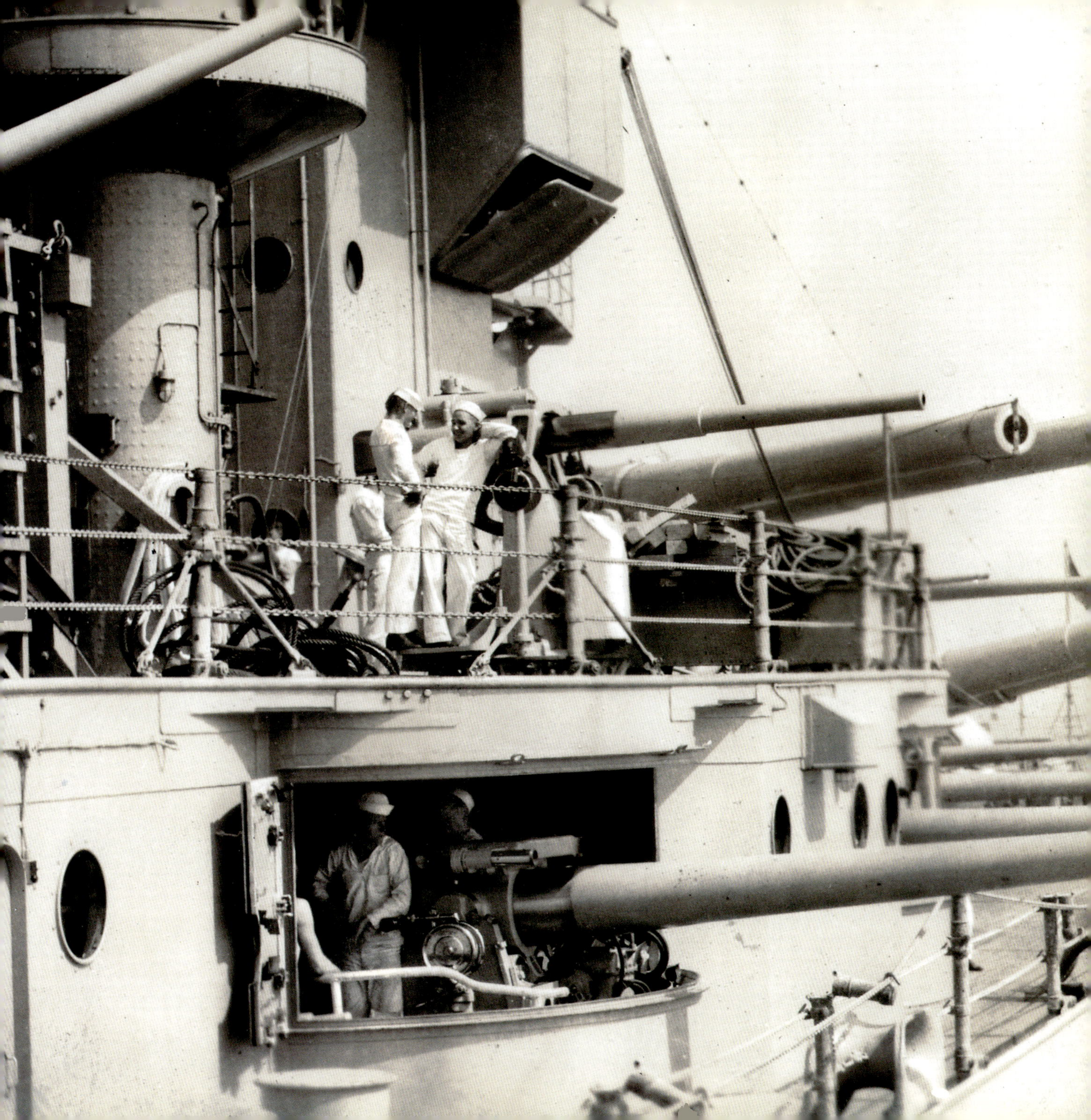

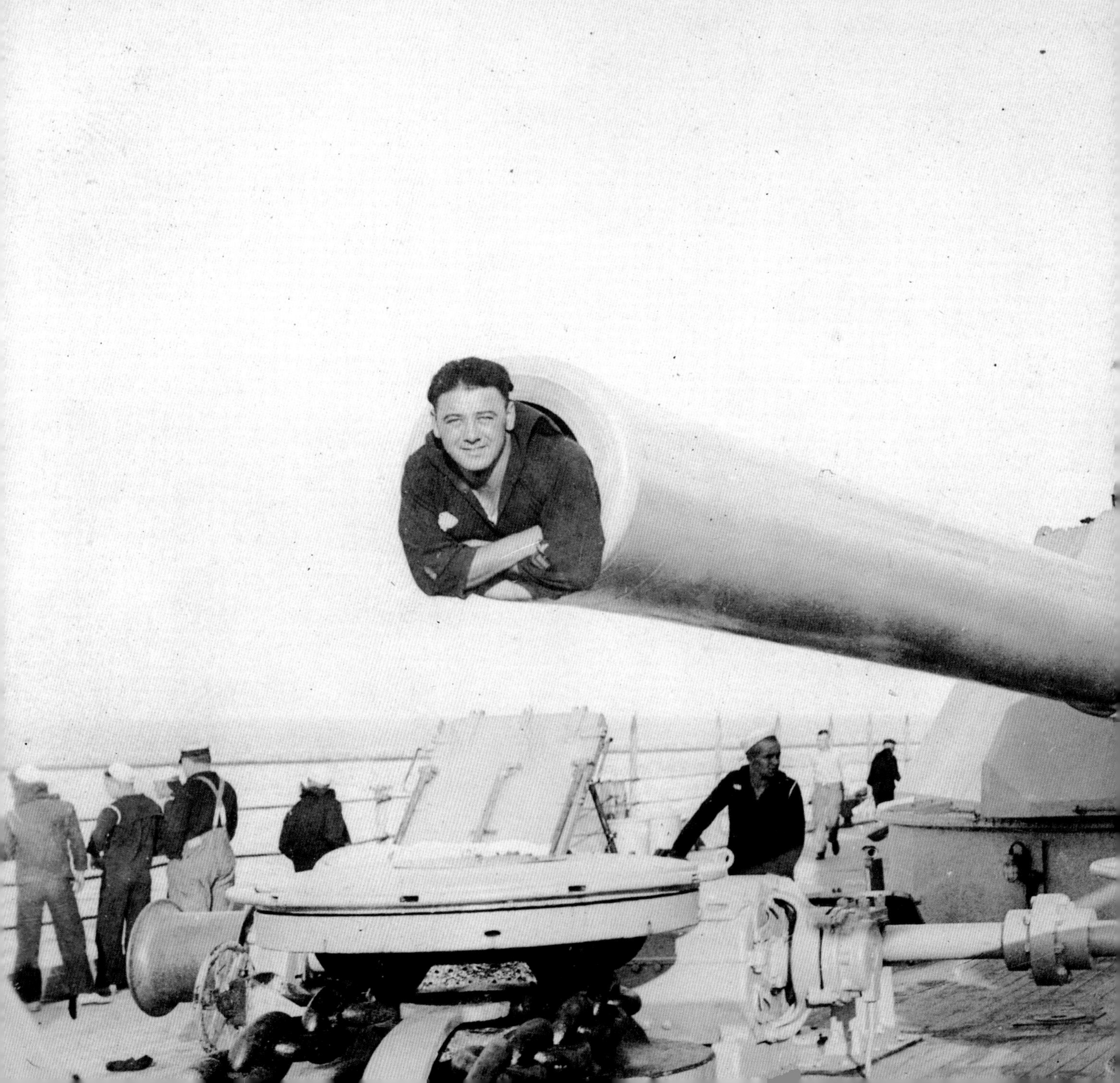

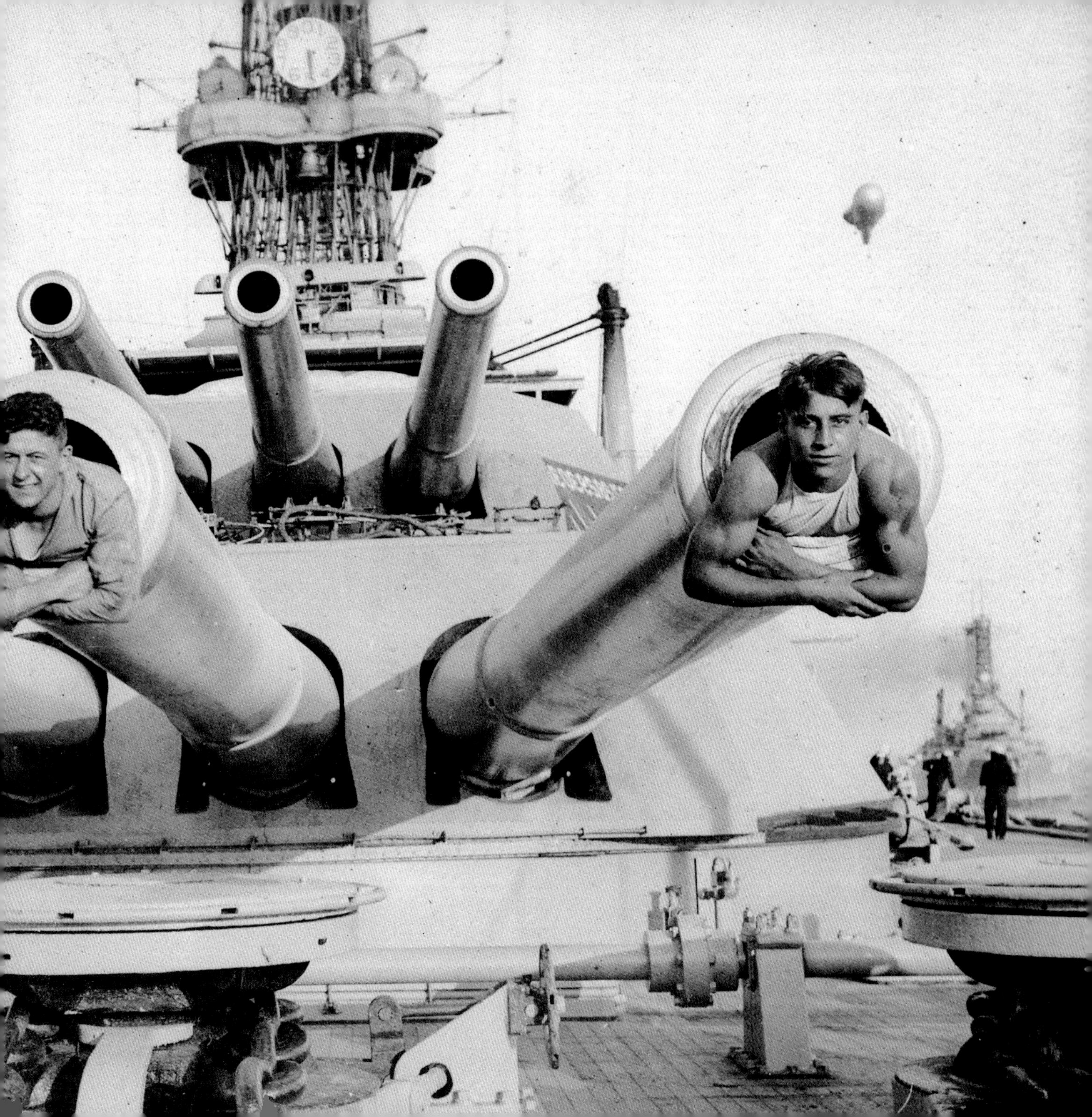

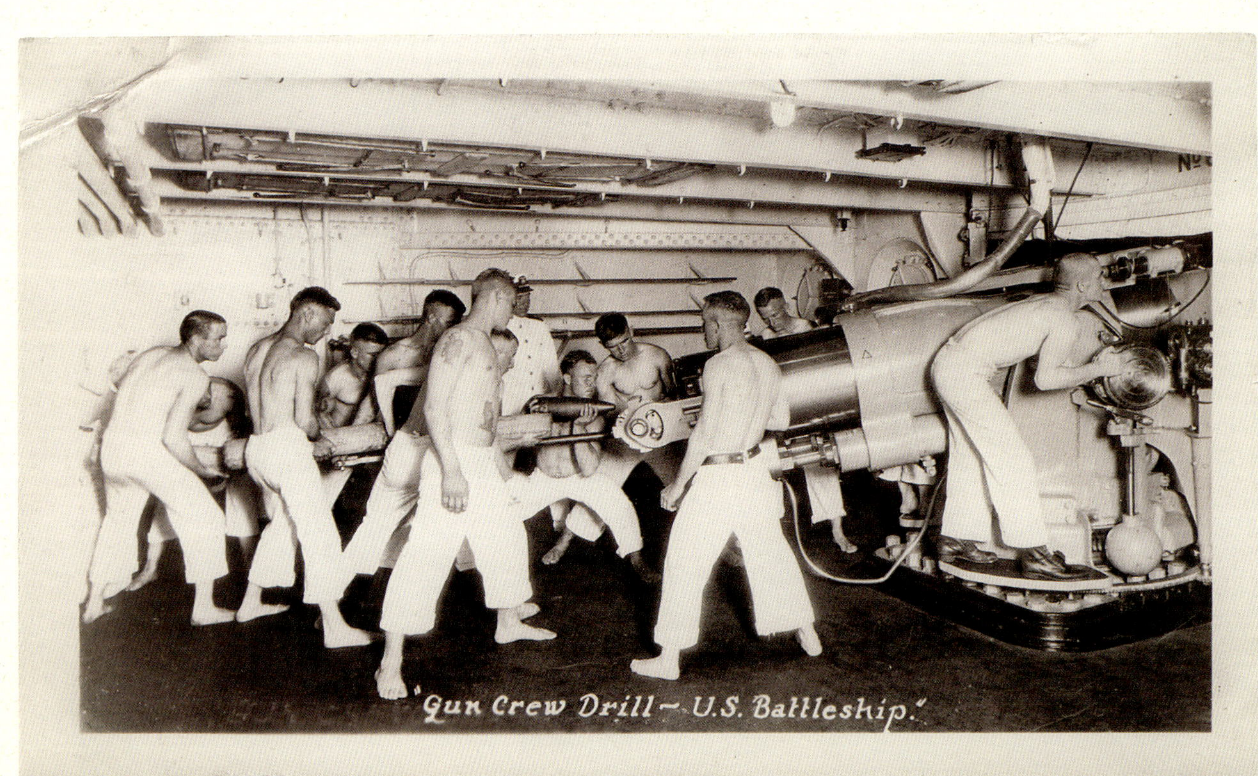

"Gun Crew Drill – U.S. Battleship."

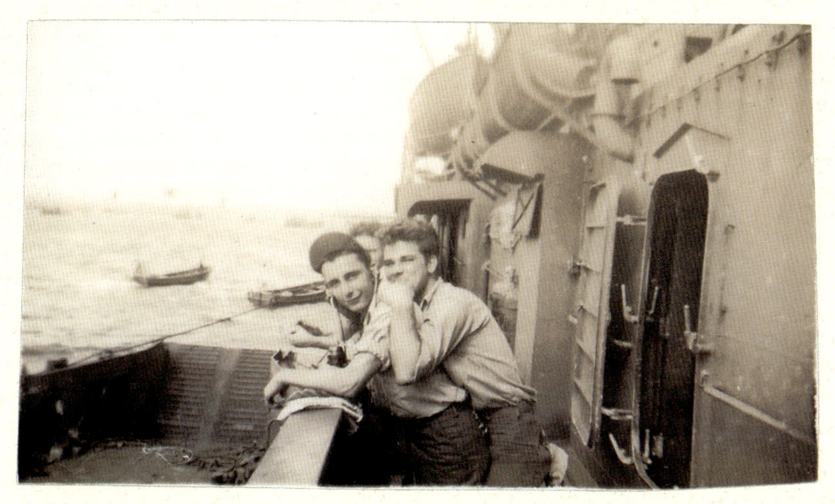

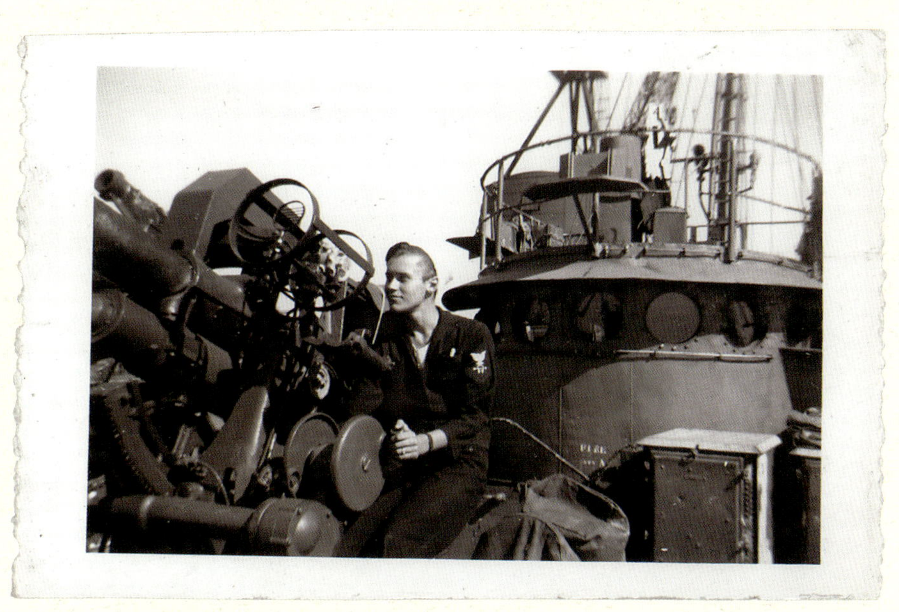

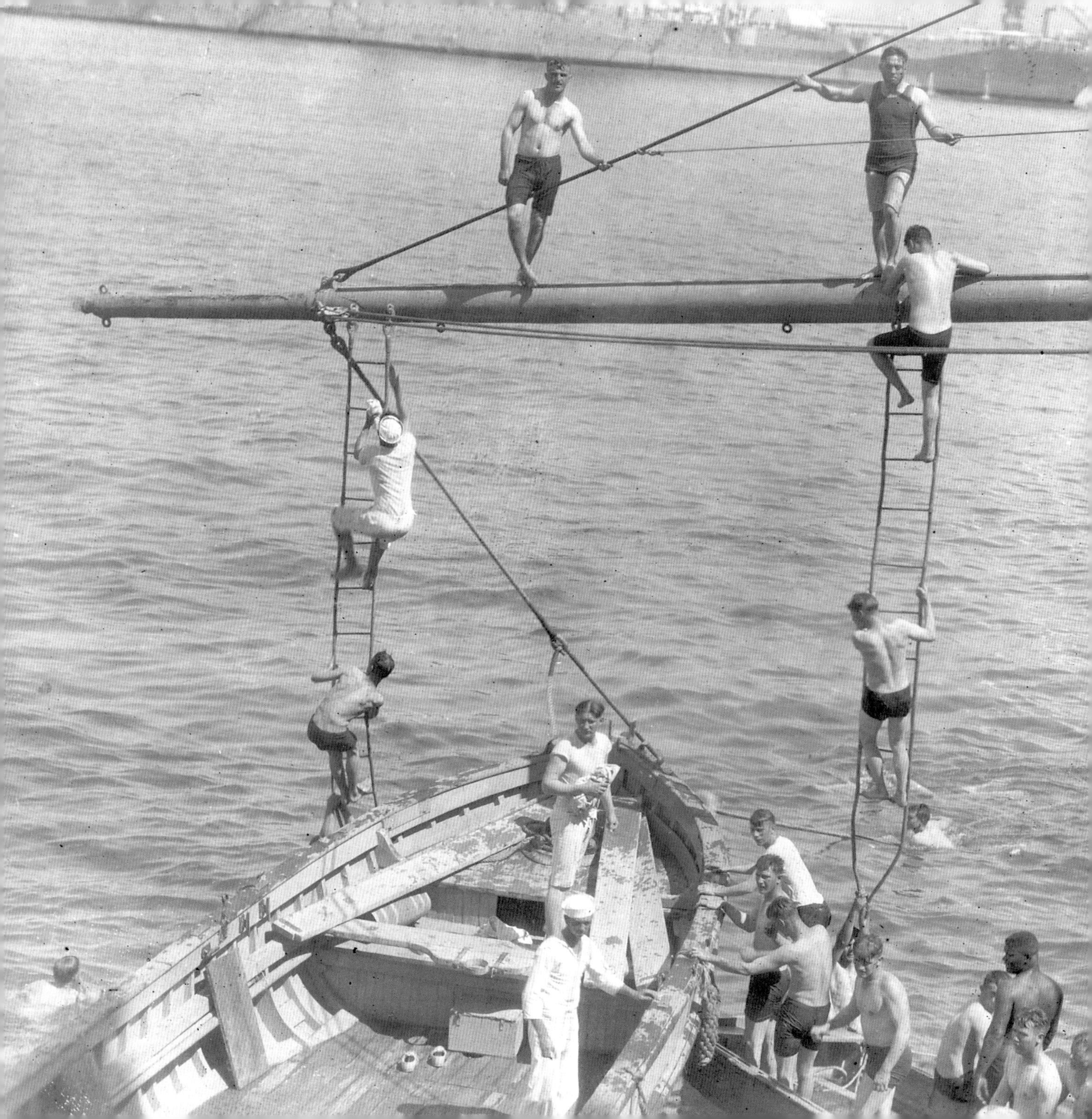

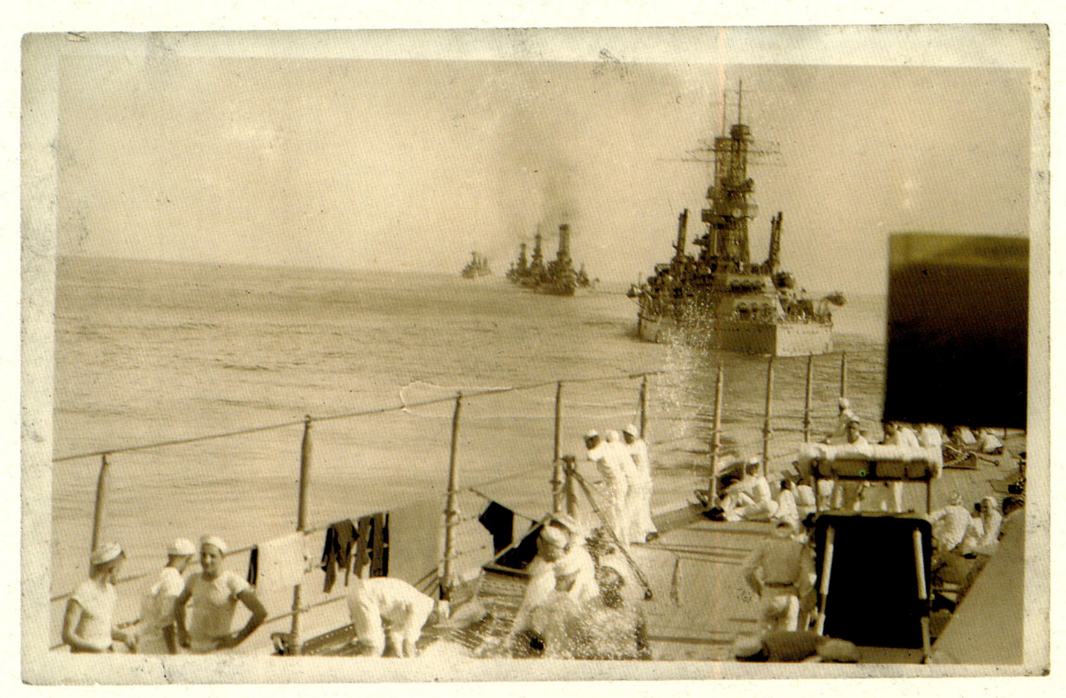

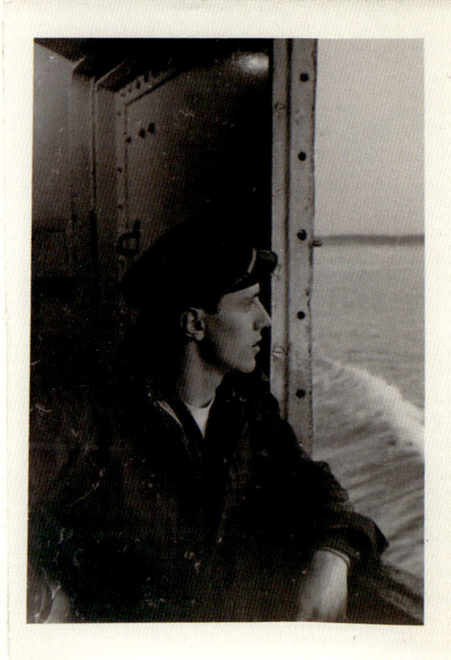

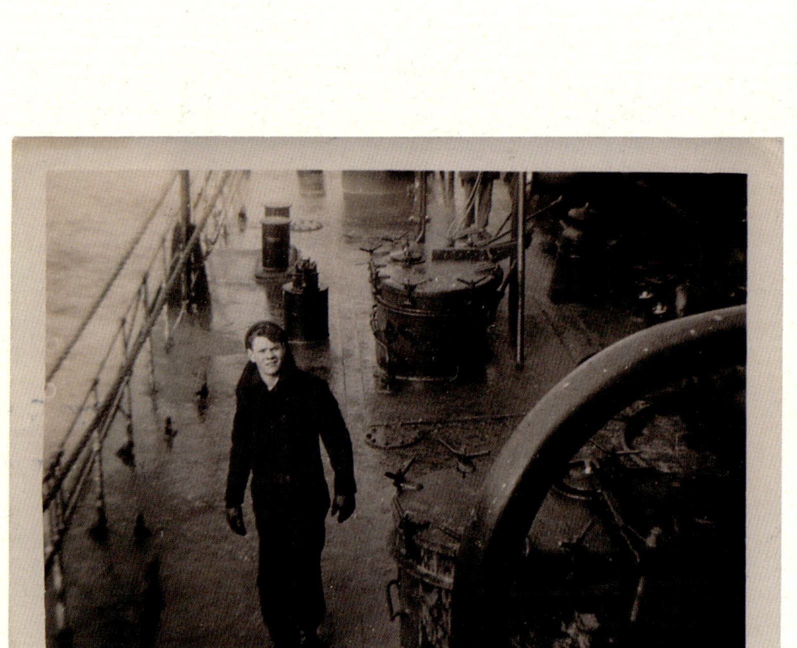

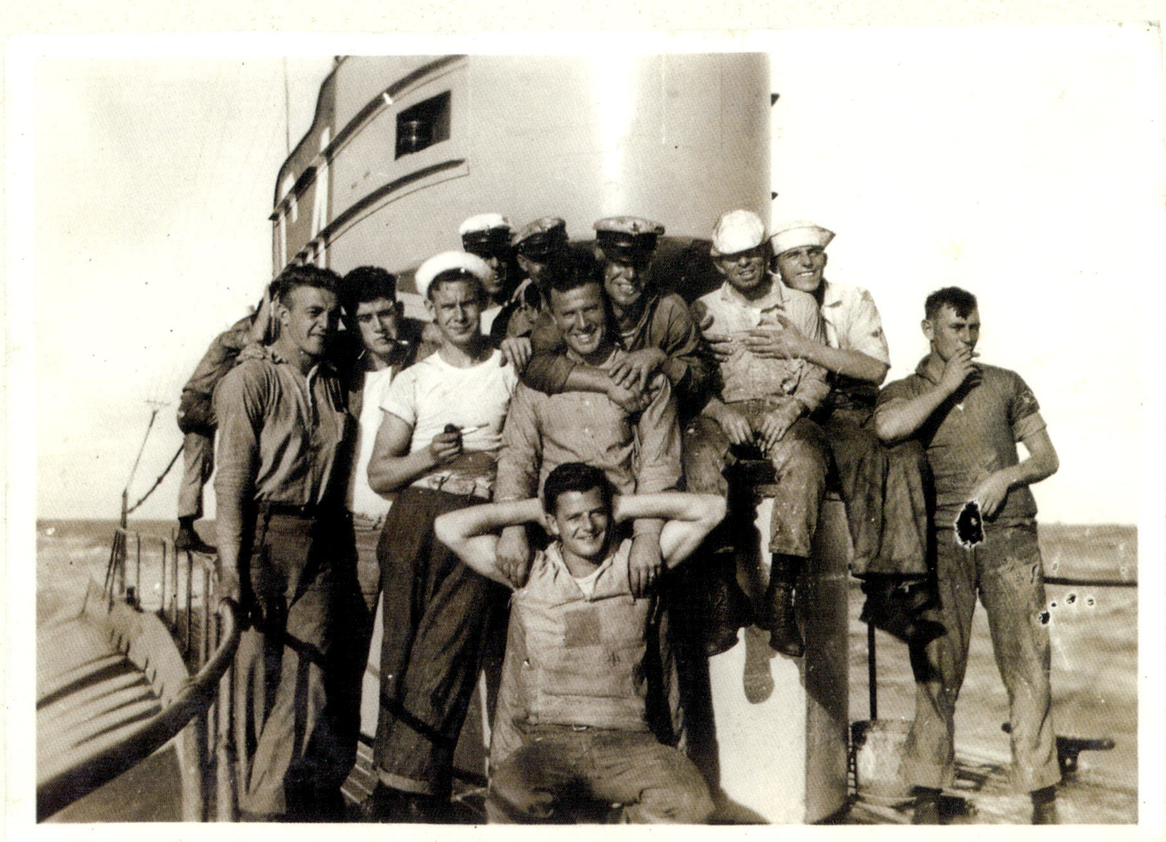

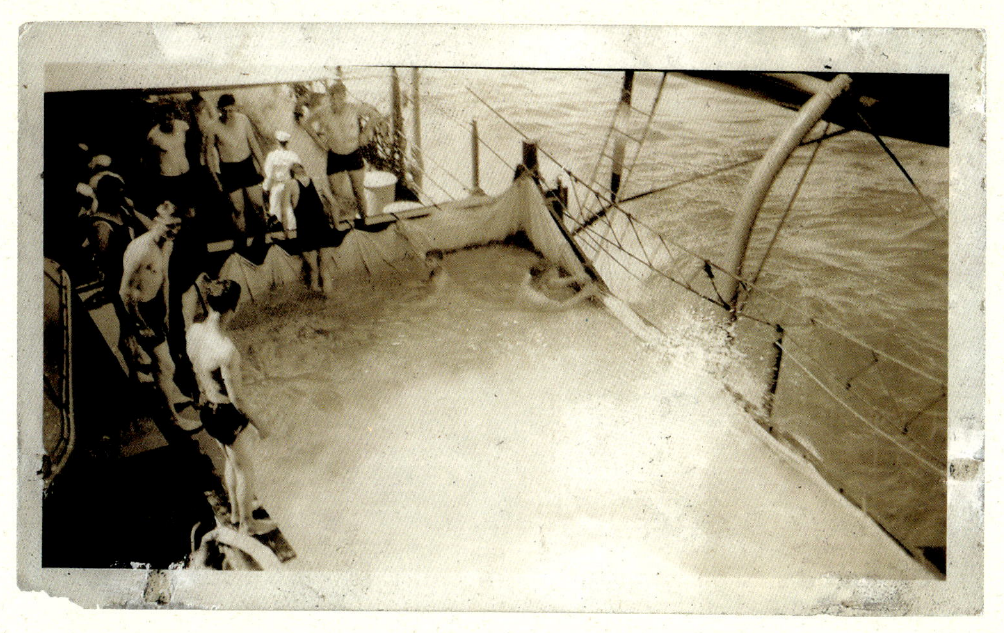

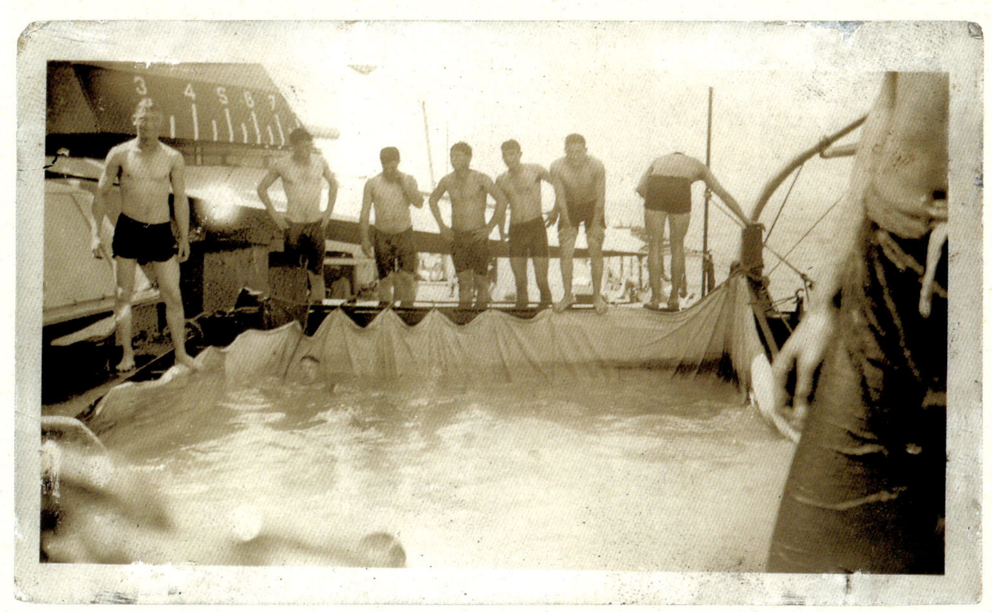
3 4 5 6 7

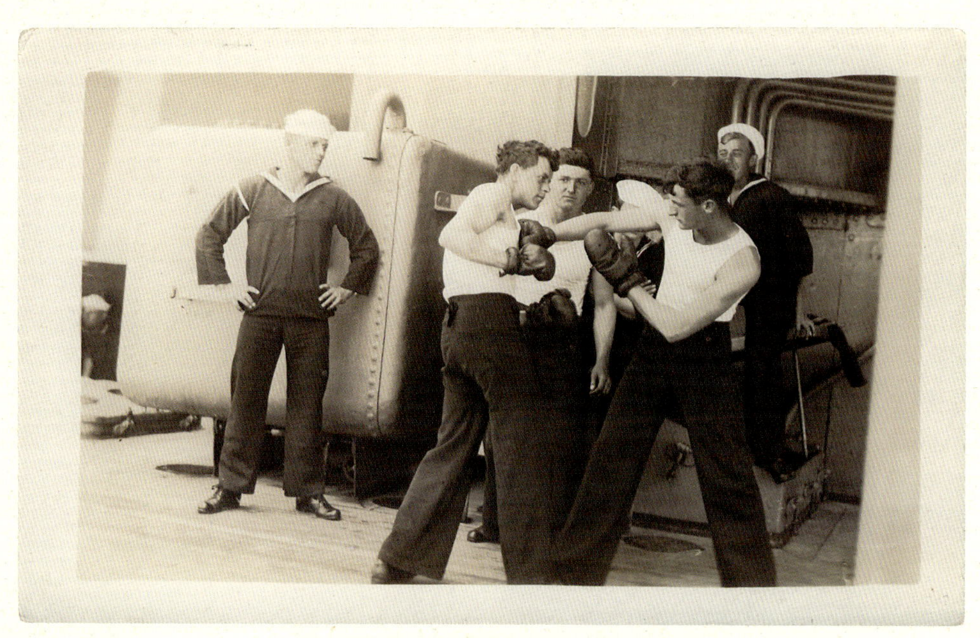

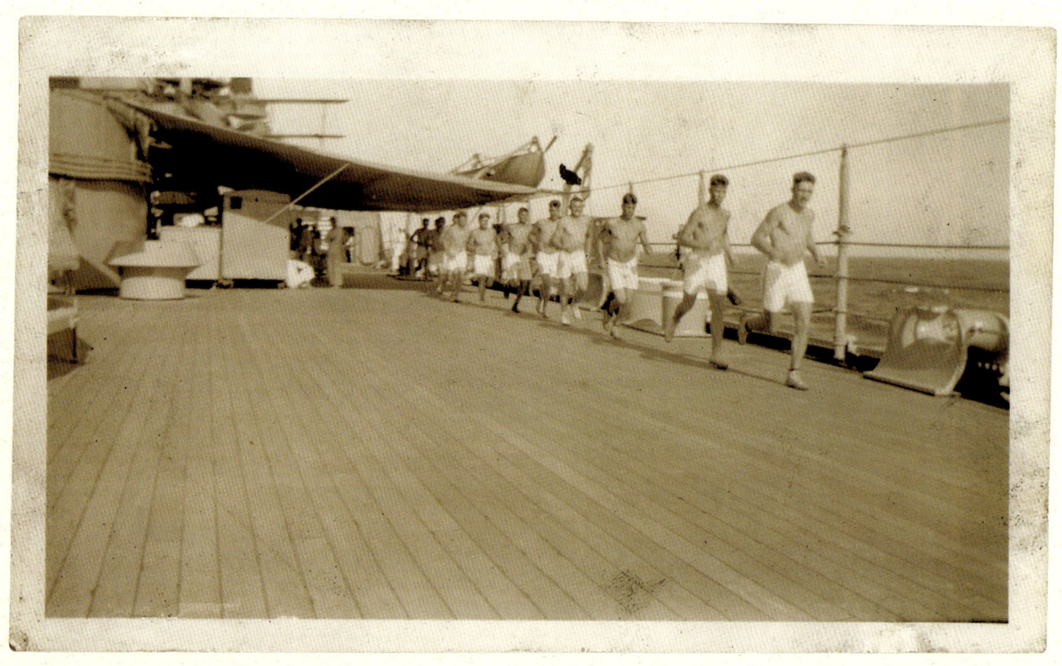

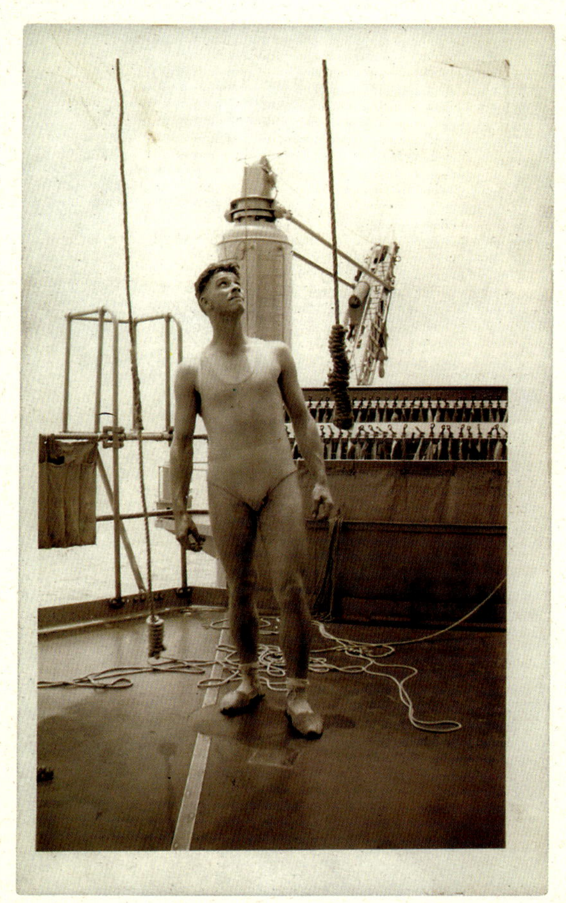

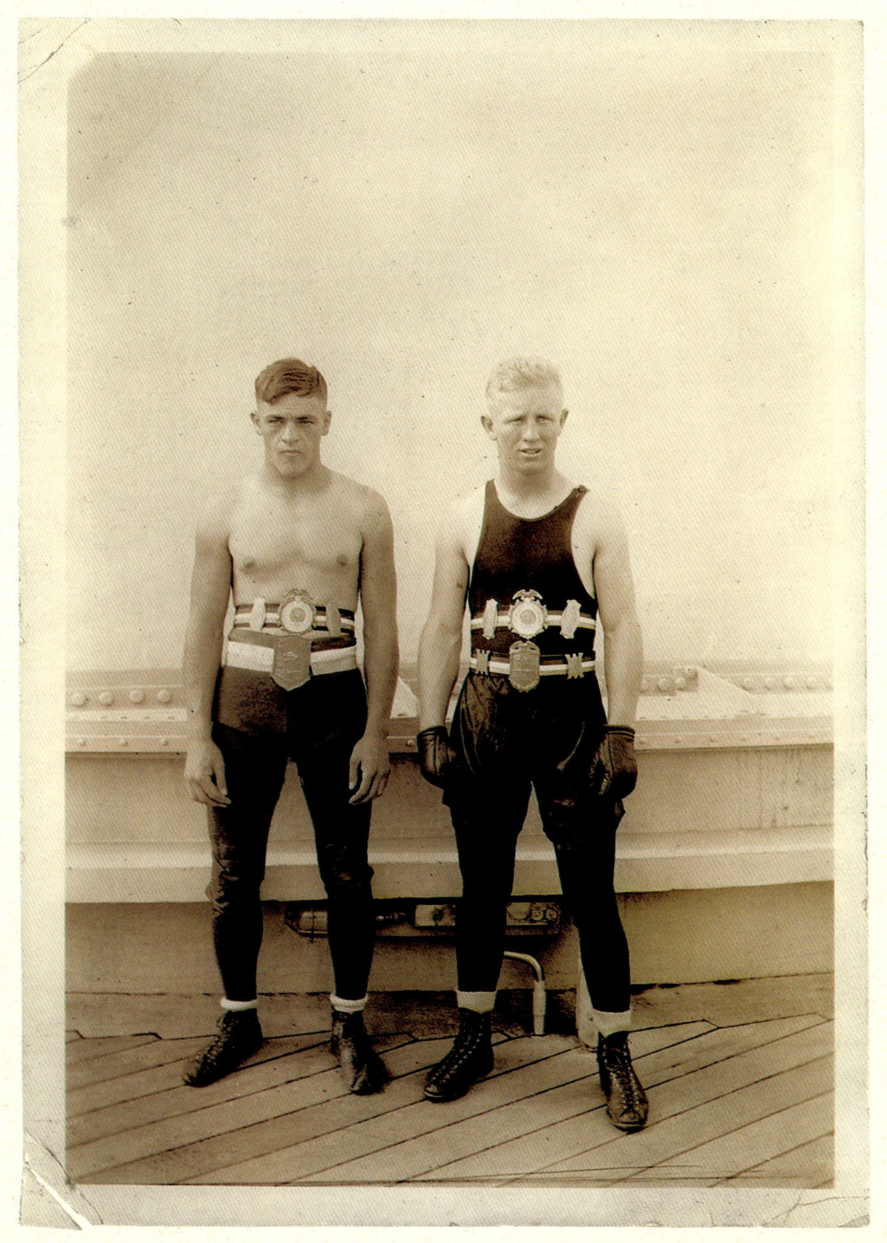

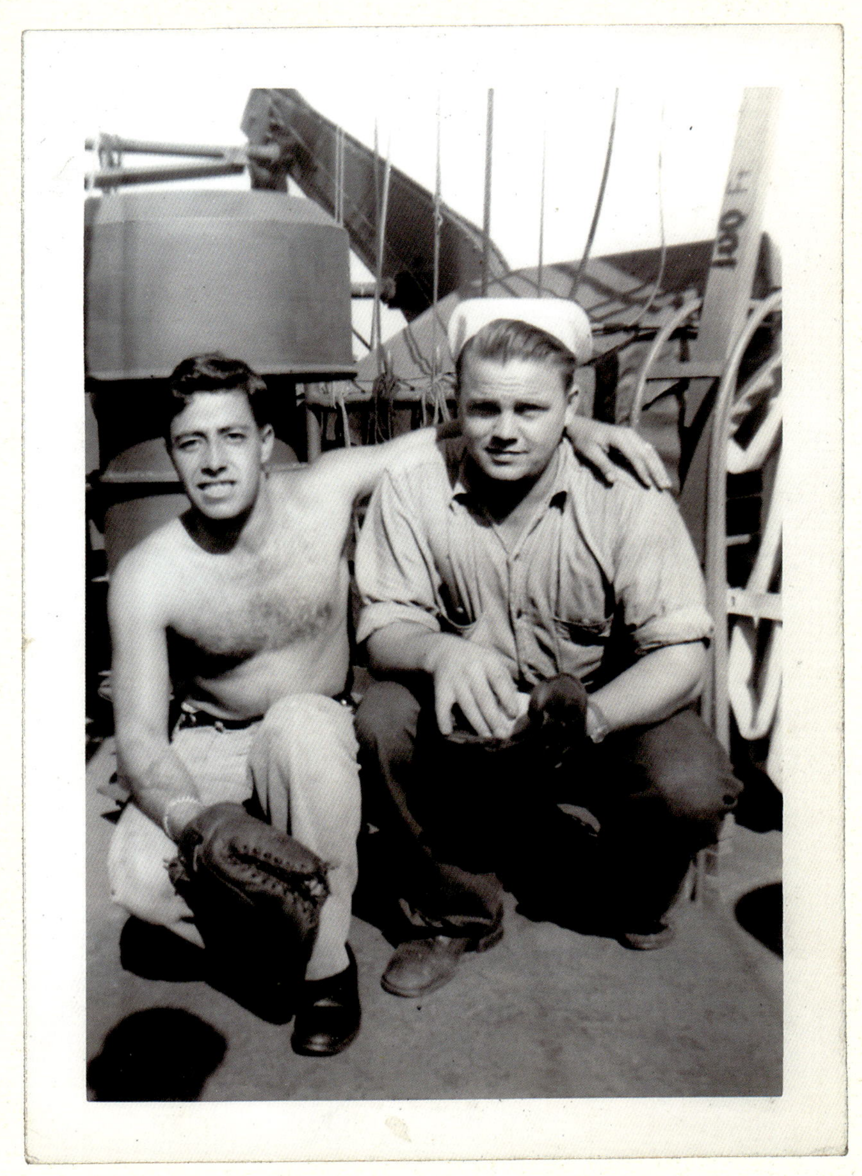

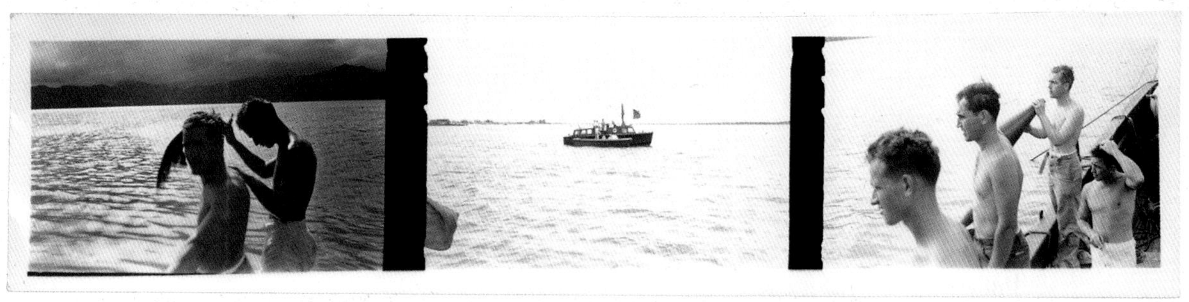

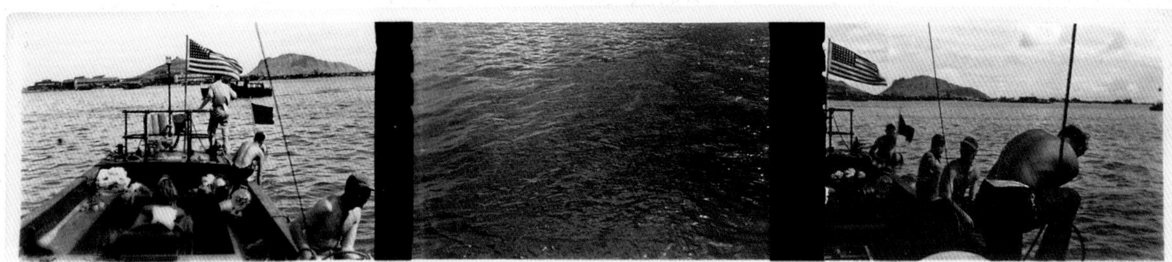

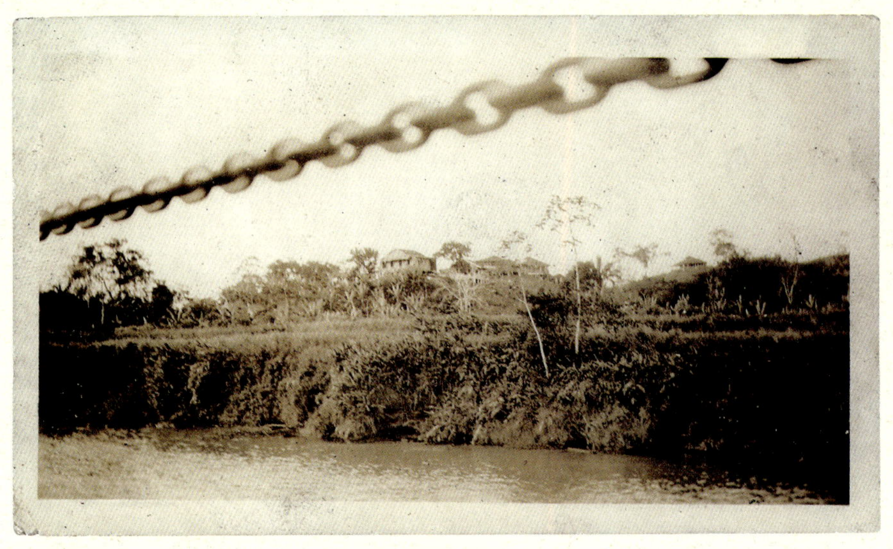

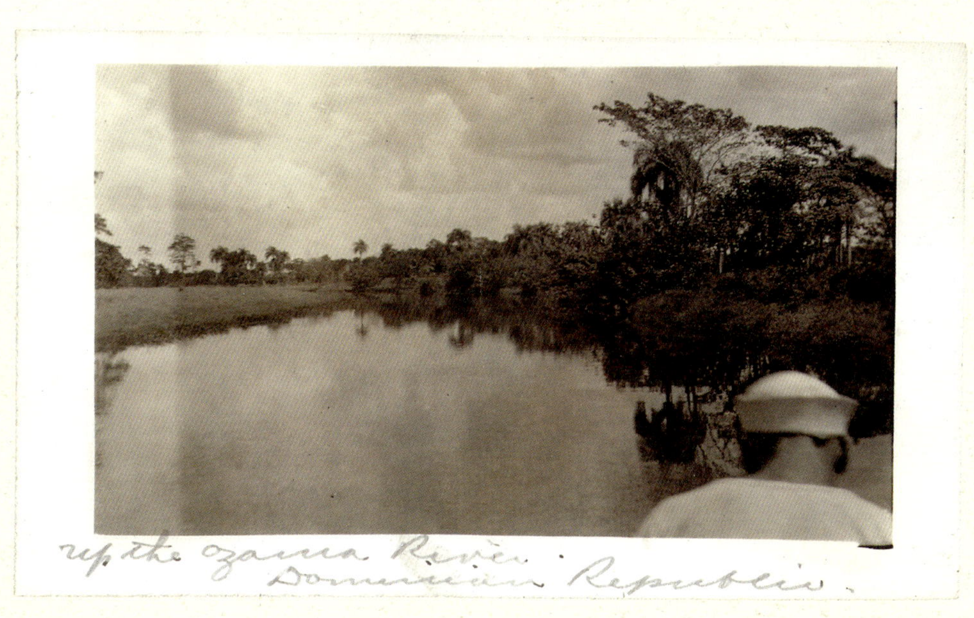

up the Ozama River.
Dominican Republic.

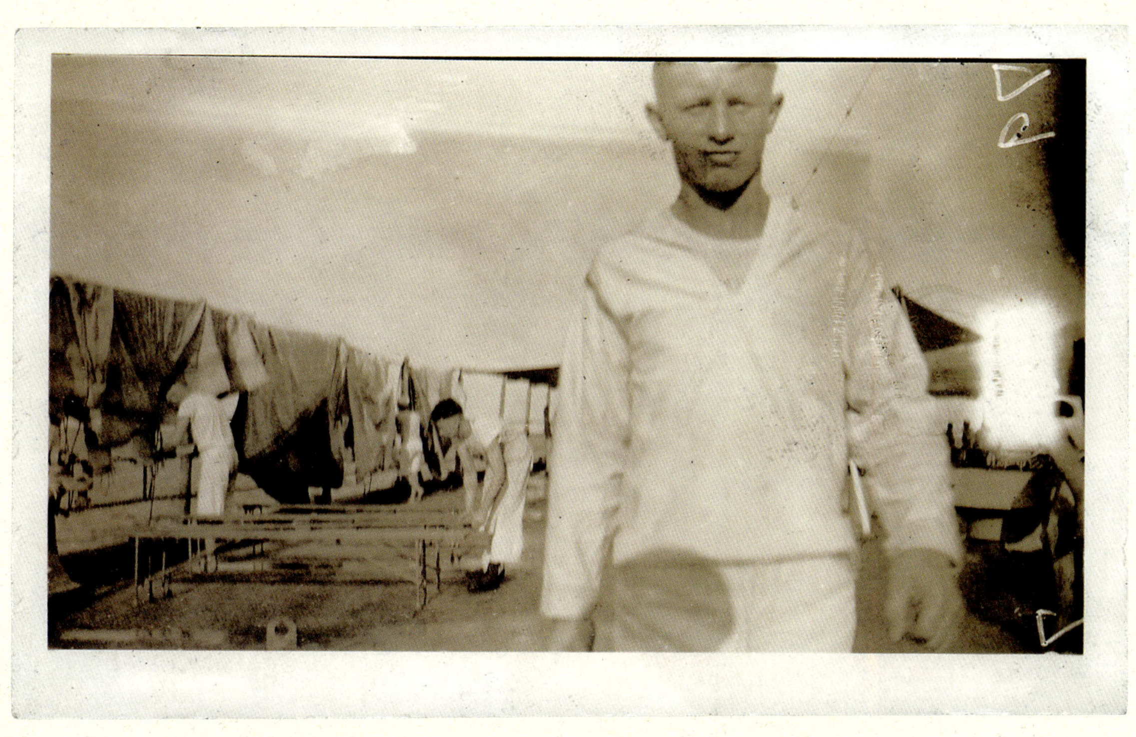

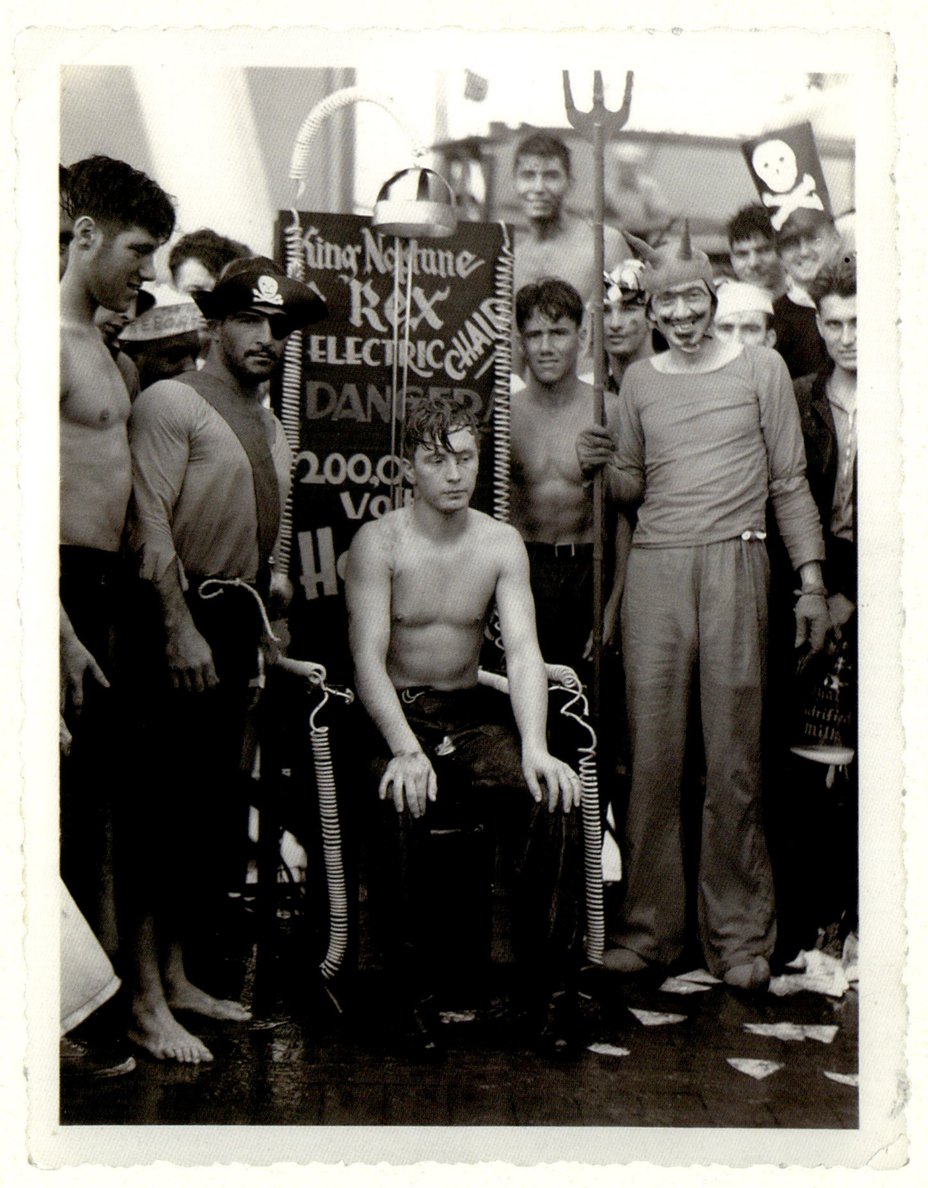
Rex
ELECTRIC

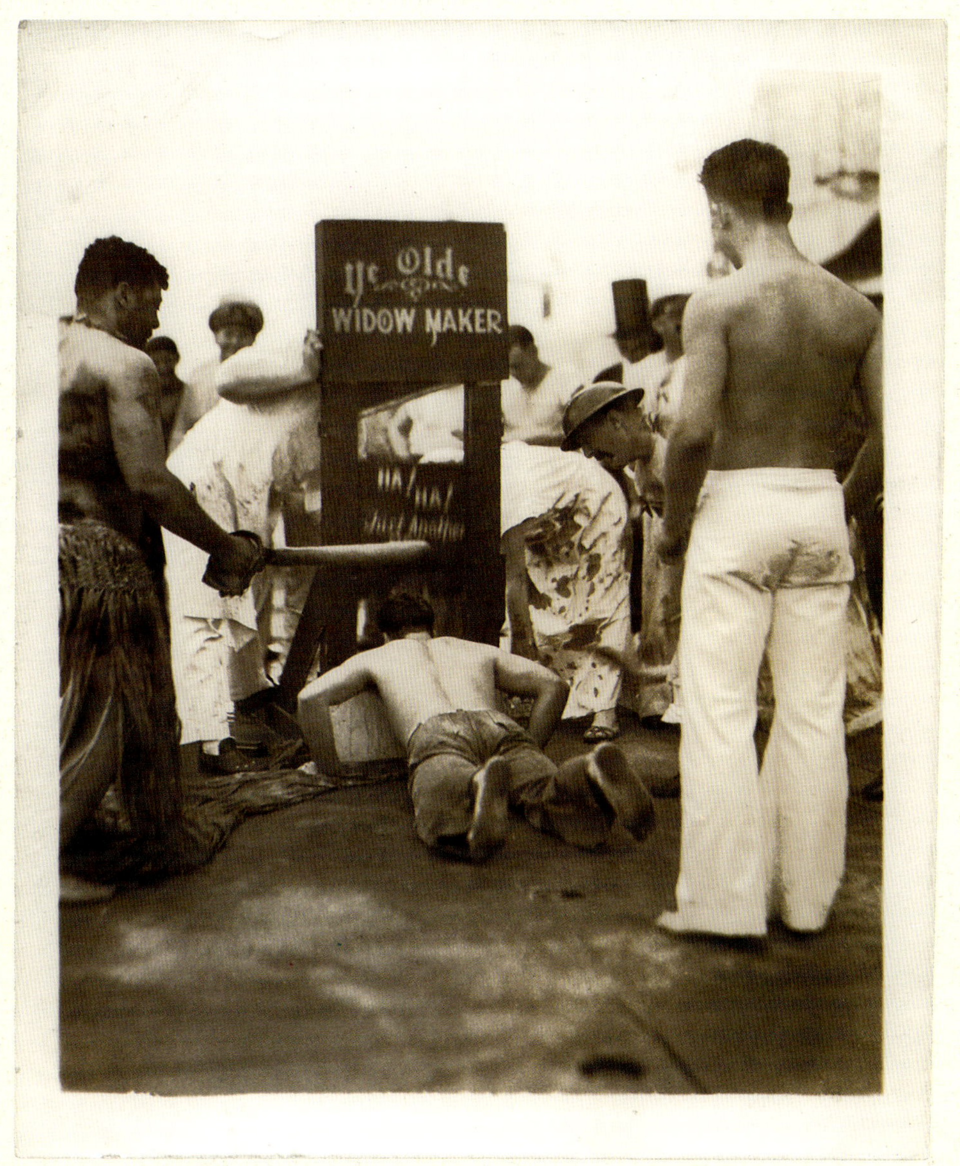
Ye Olde
WIDOW MAKER
HA! HA!
Just Another

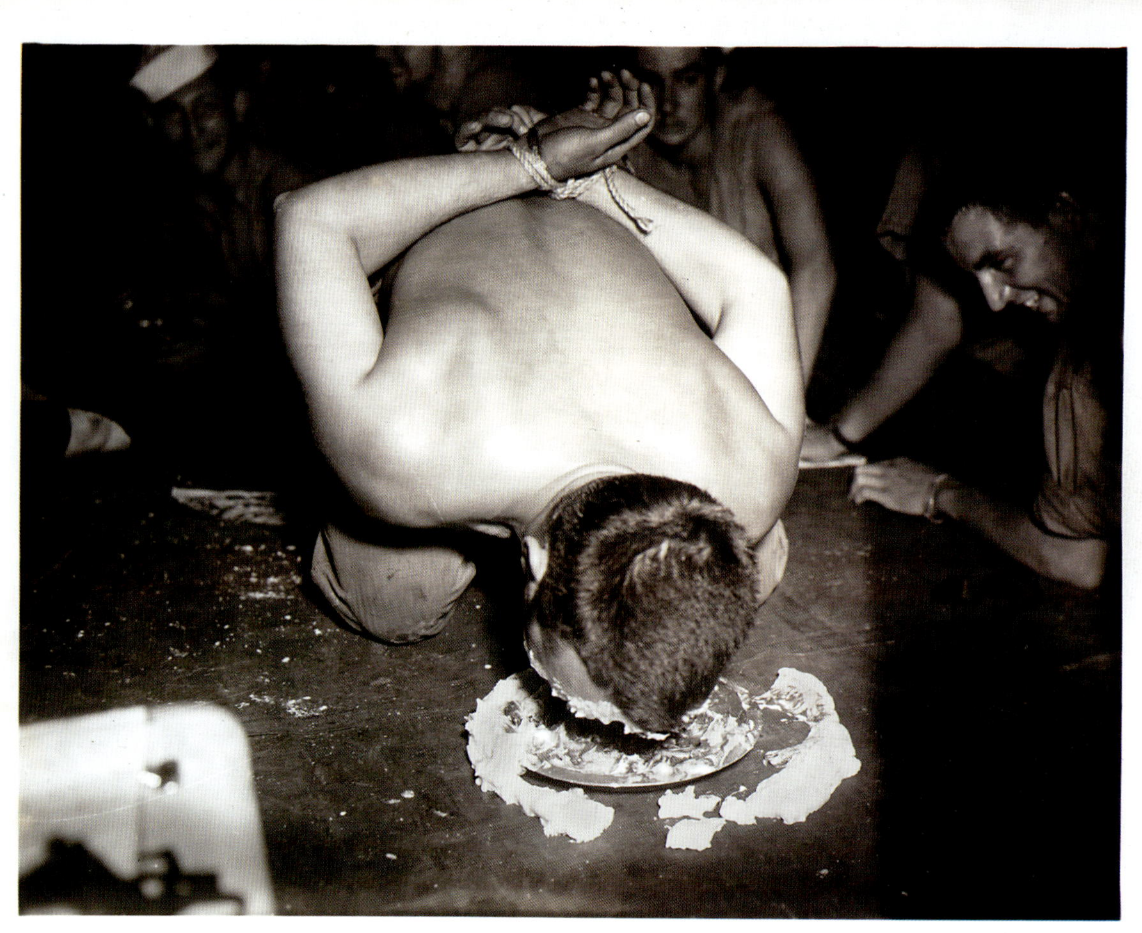

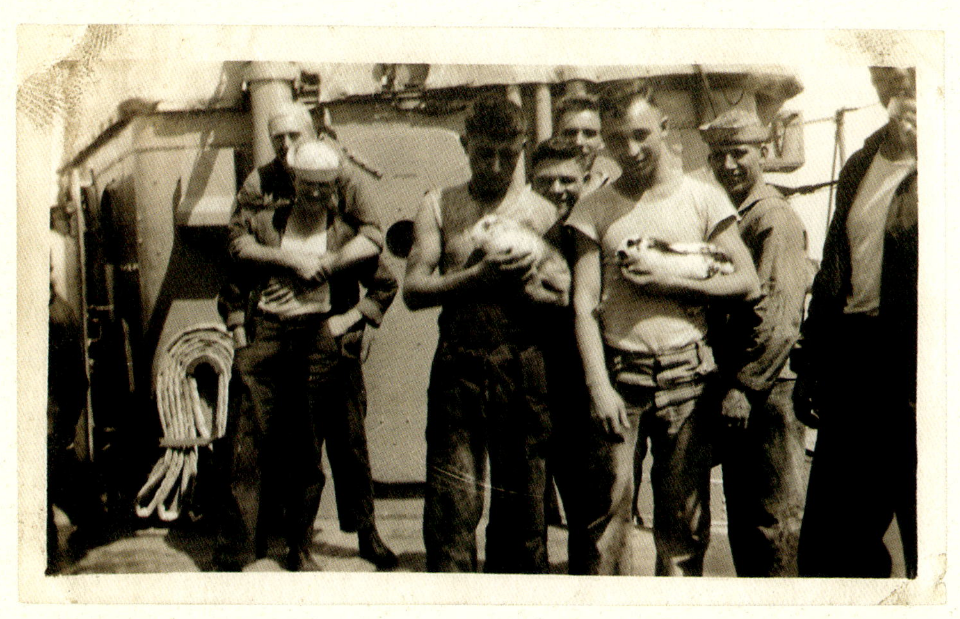

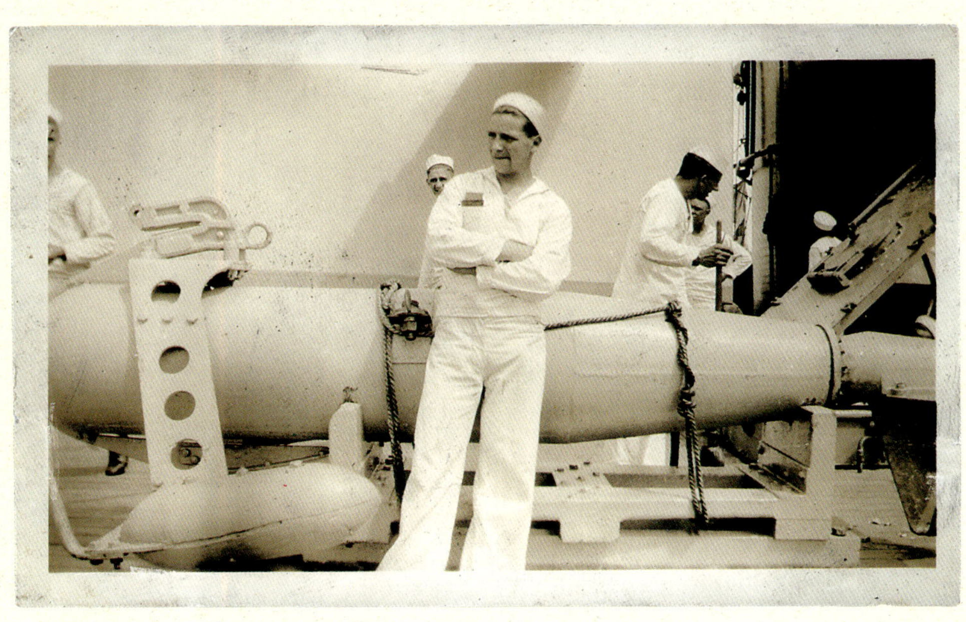

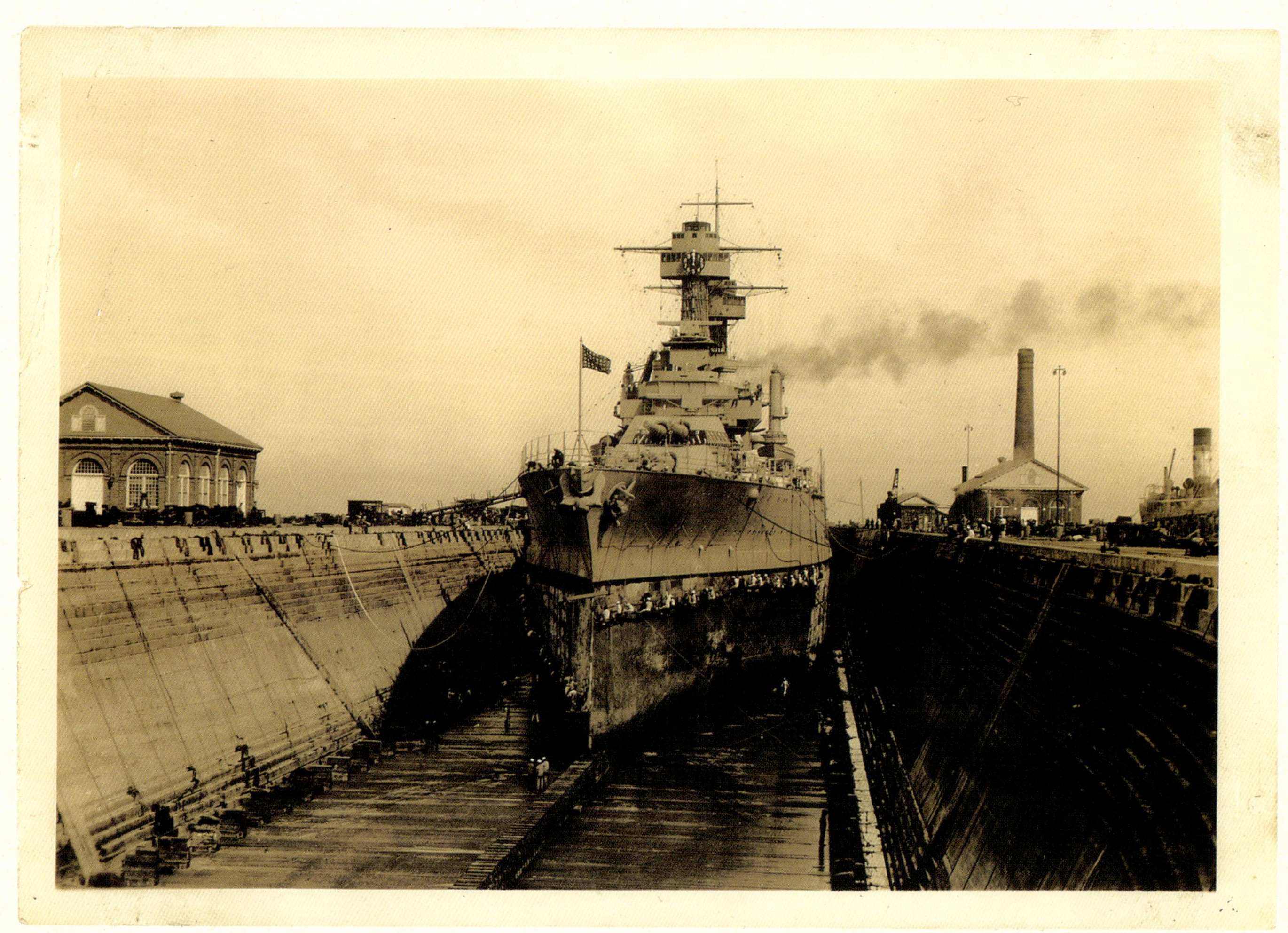

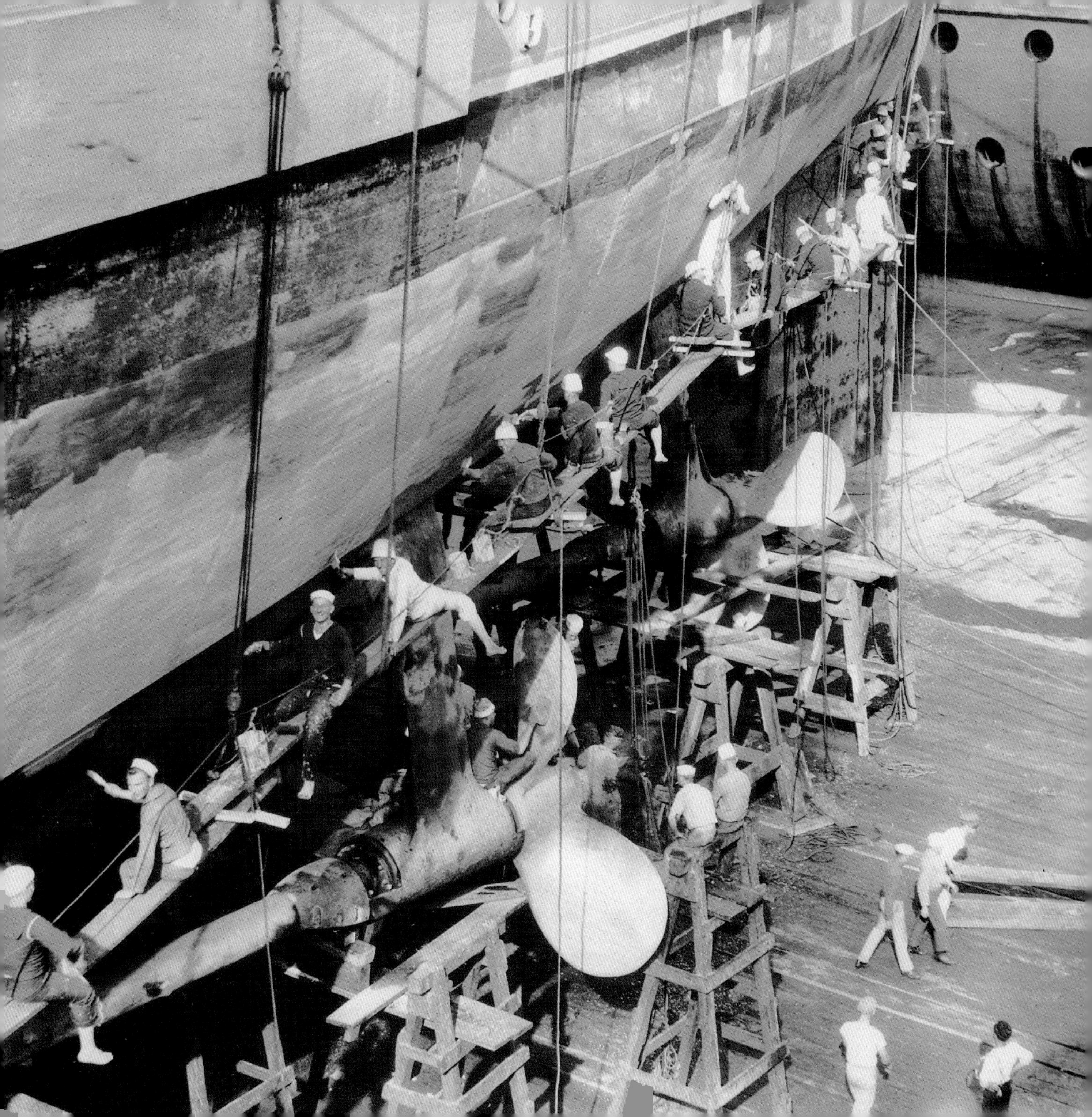

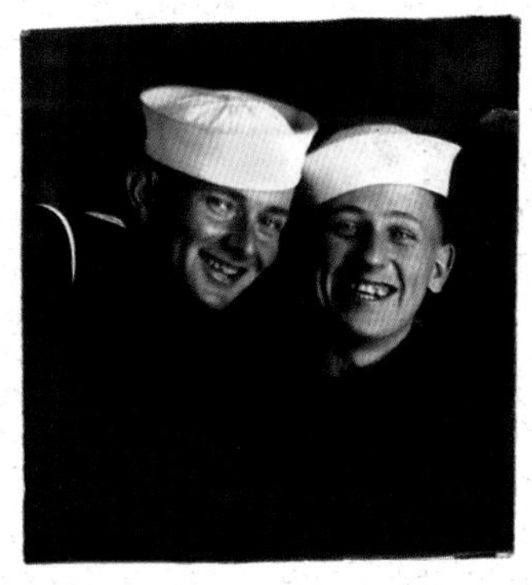

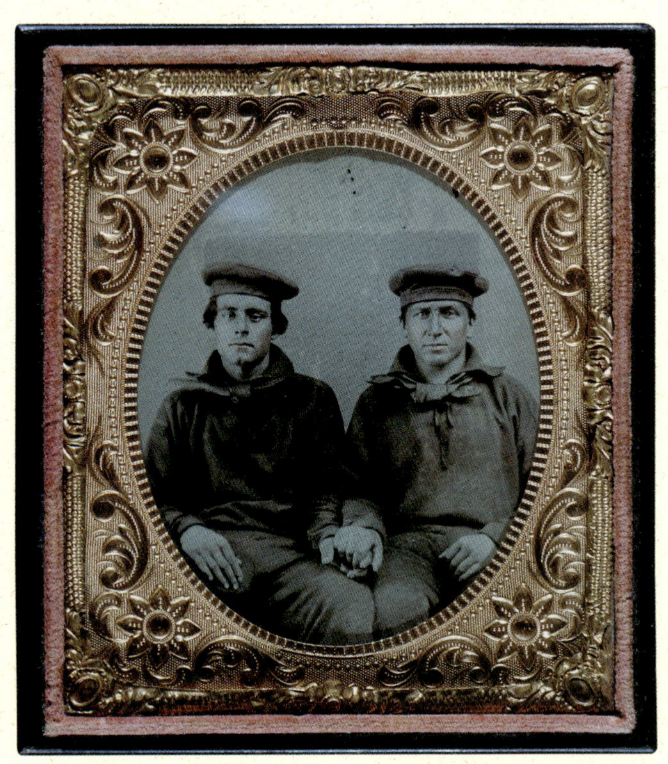

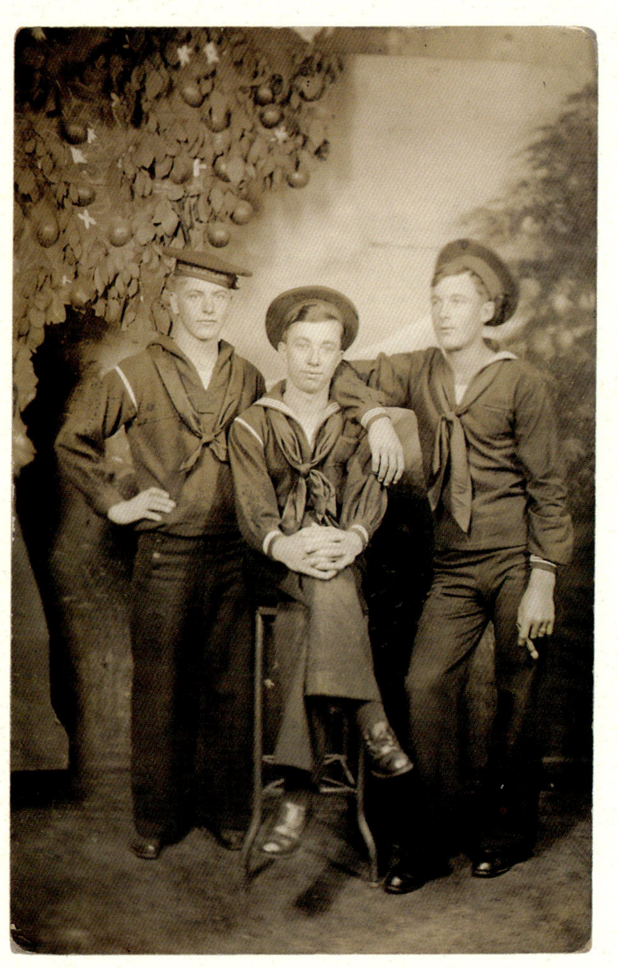

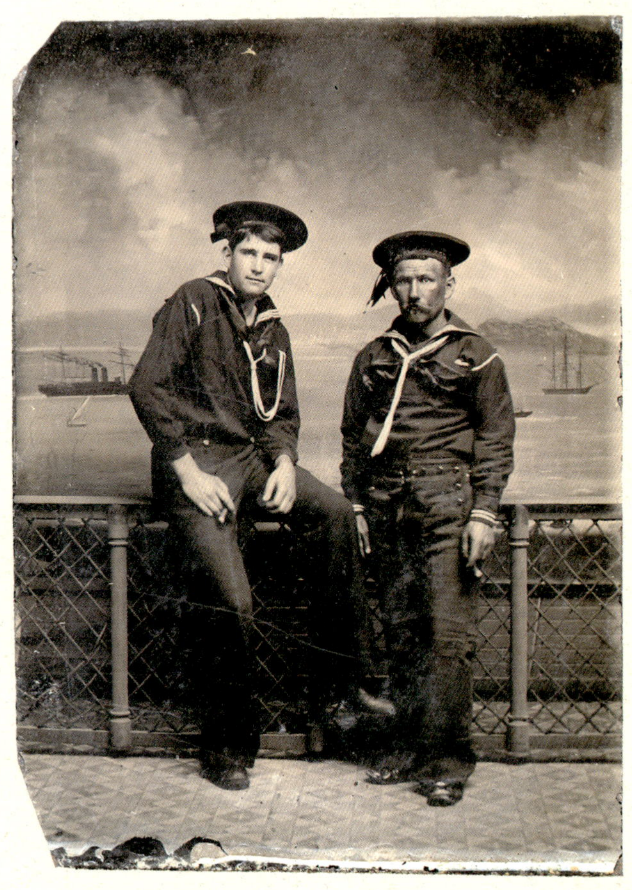

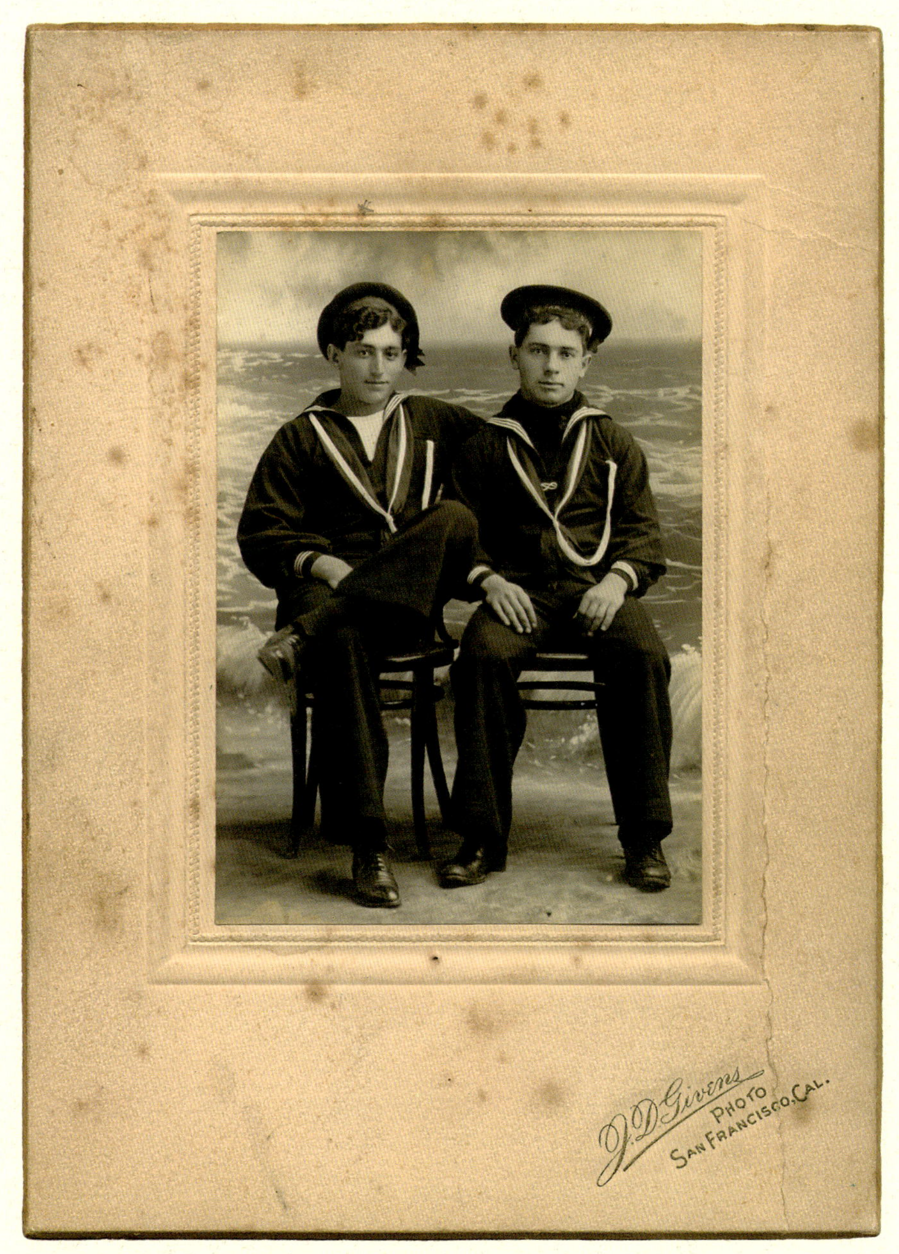
J. D. Givens
PHOTO
SAN FRANCISCO, CAL.

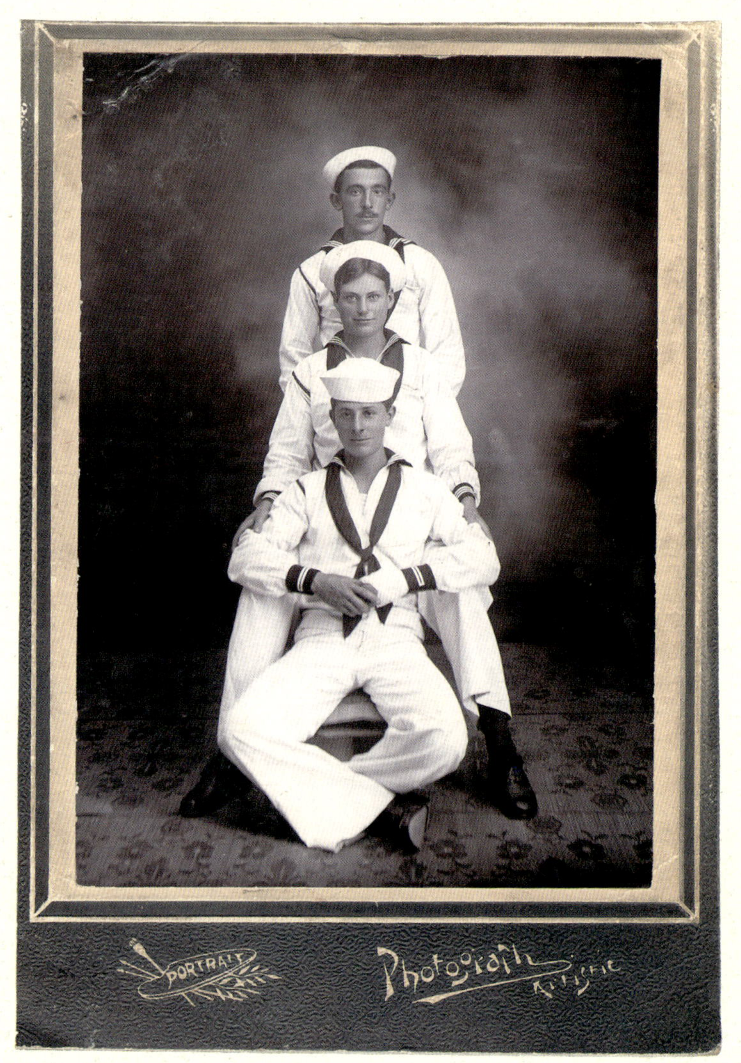
PORTRAIT
Photograph
Artistic

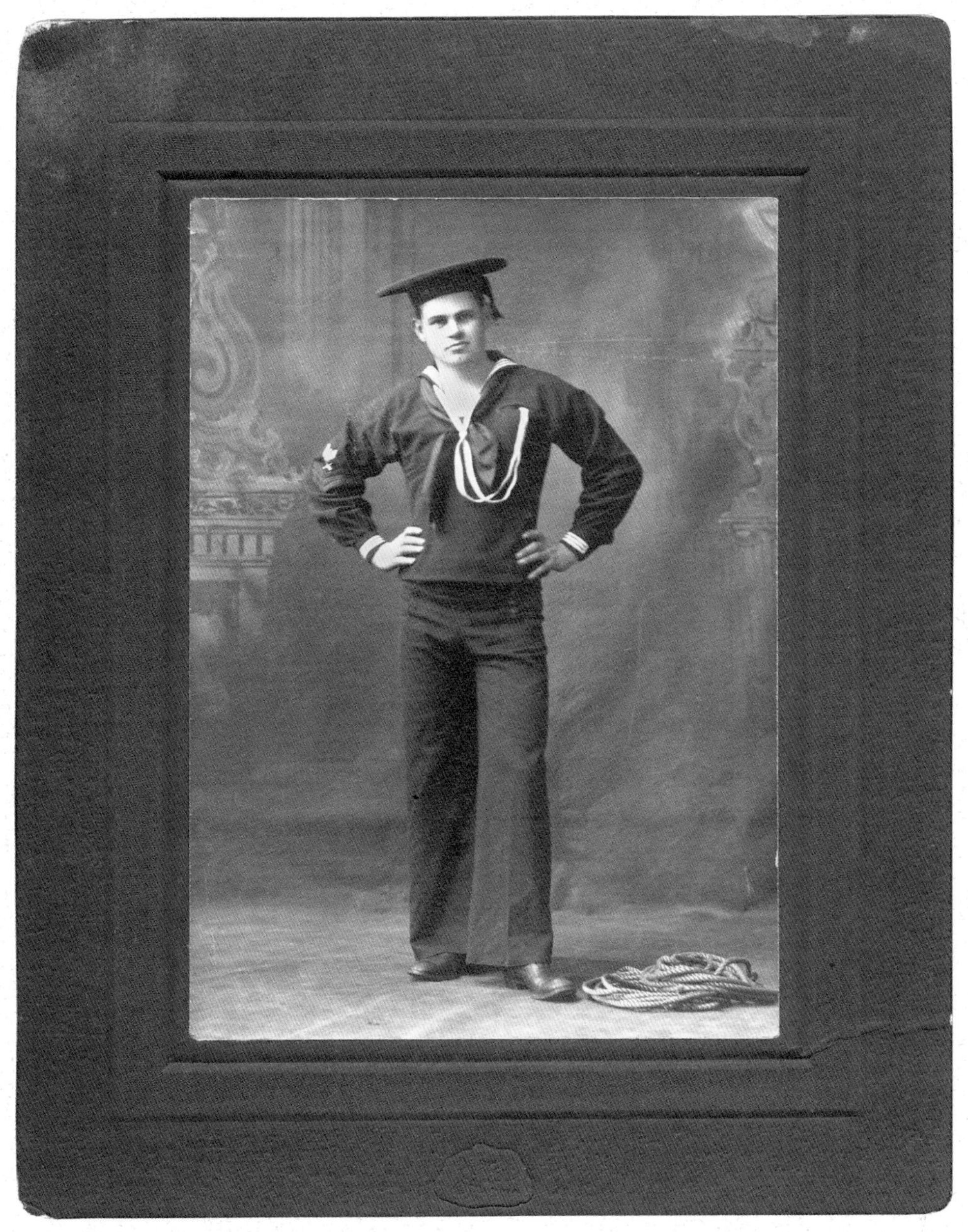

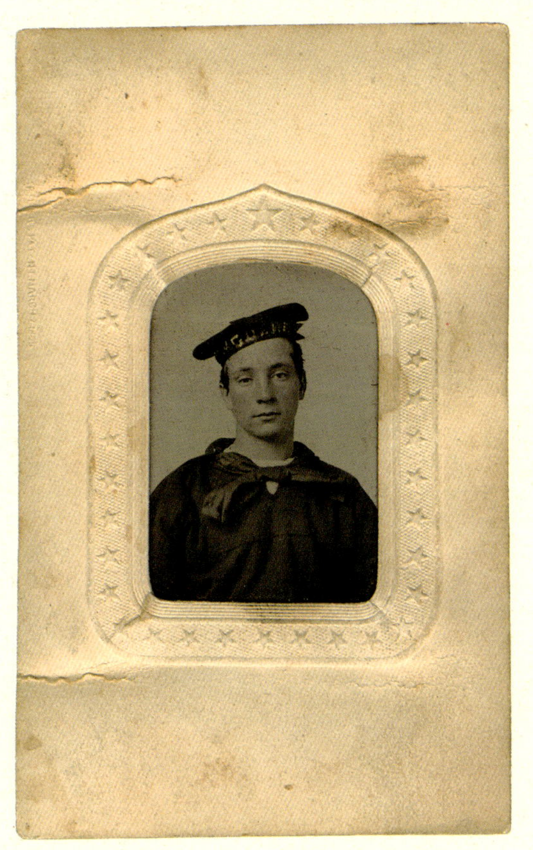

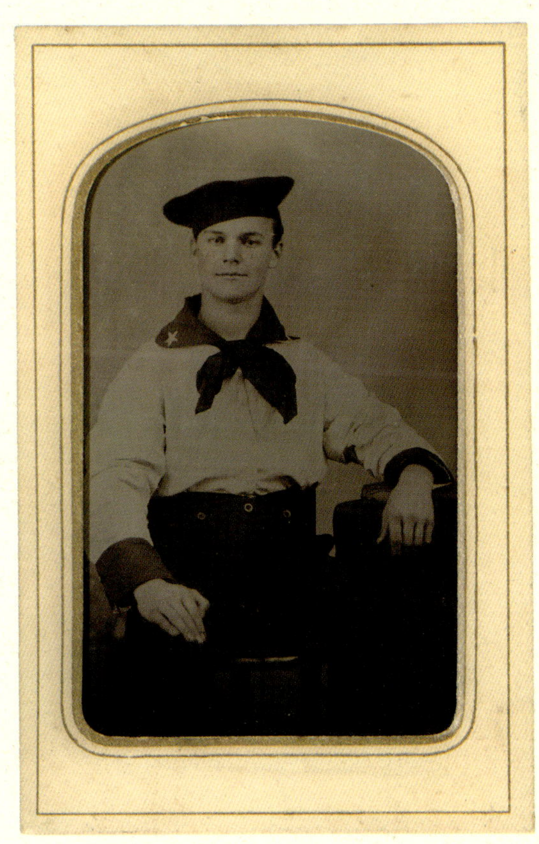

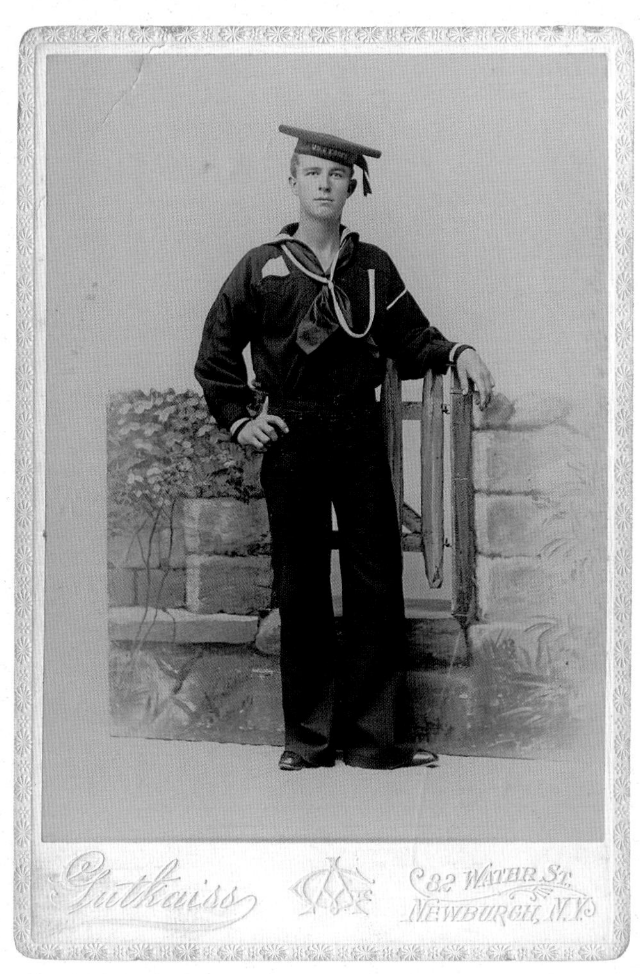
Guthaiss
82 Water St.
Newburgh, N.Y.

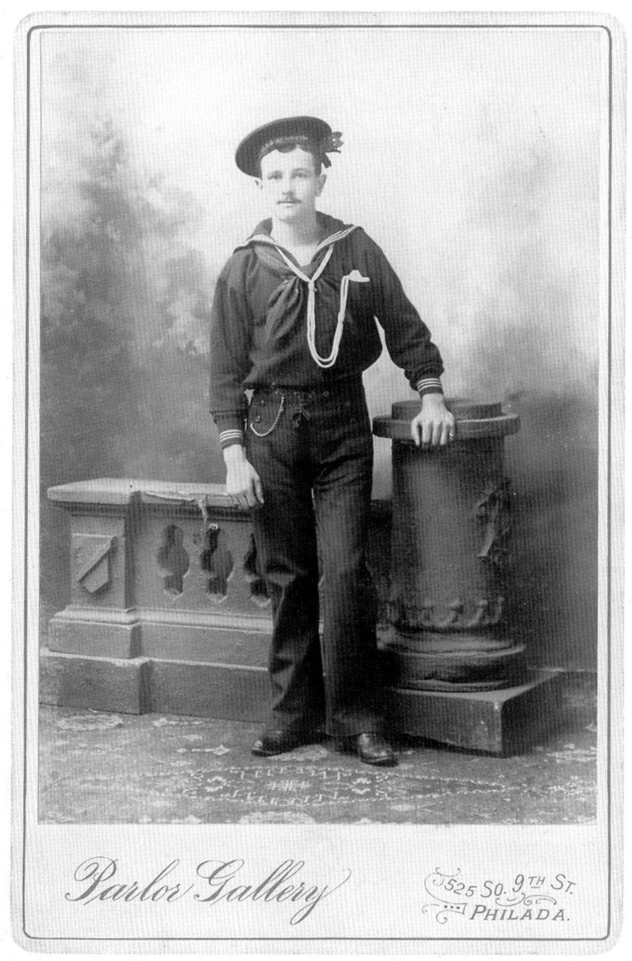
Parlor Gallery
525 So. 9TH St.
PHILADA.

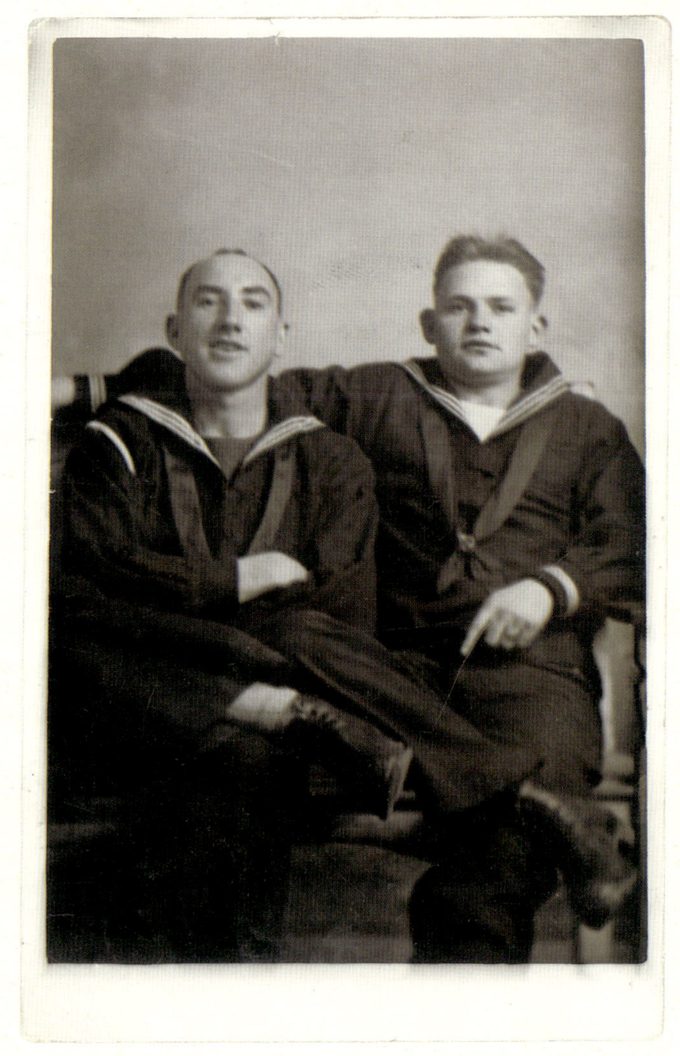

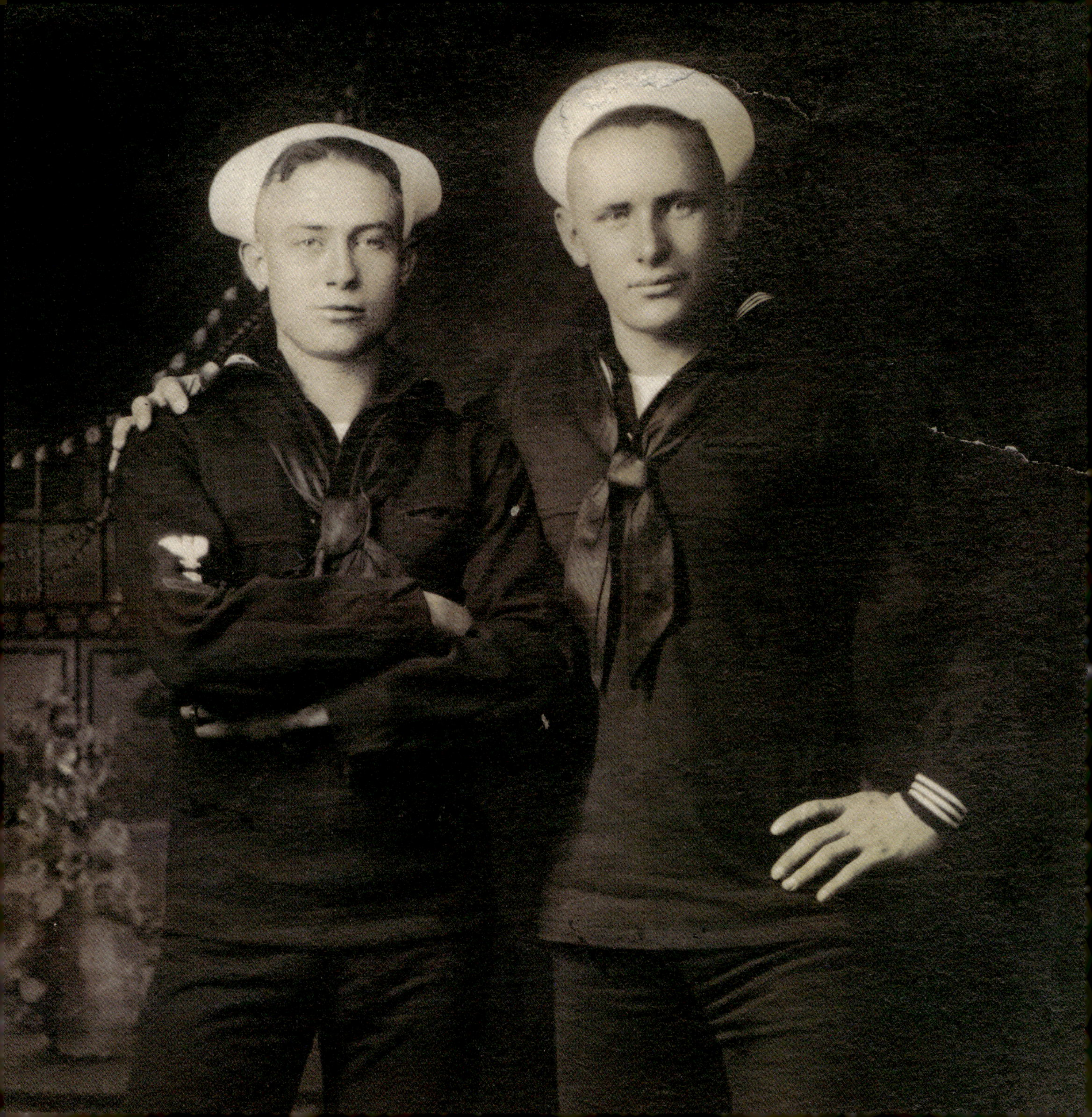

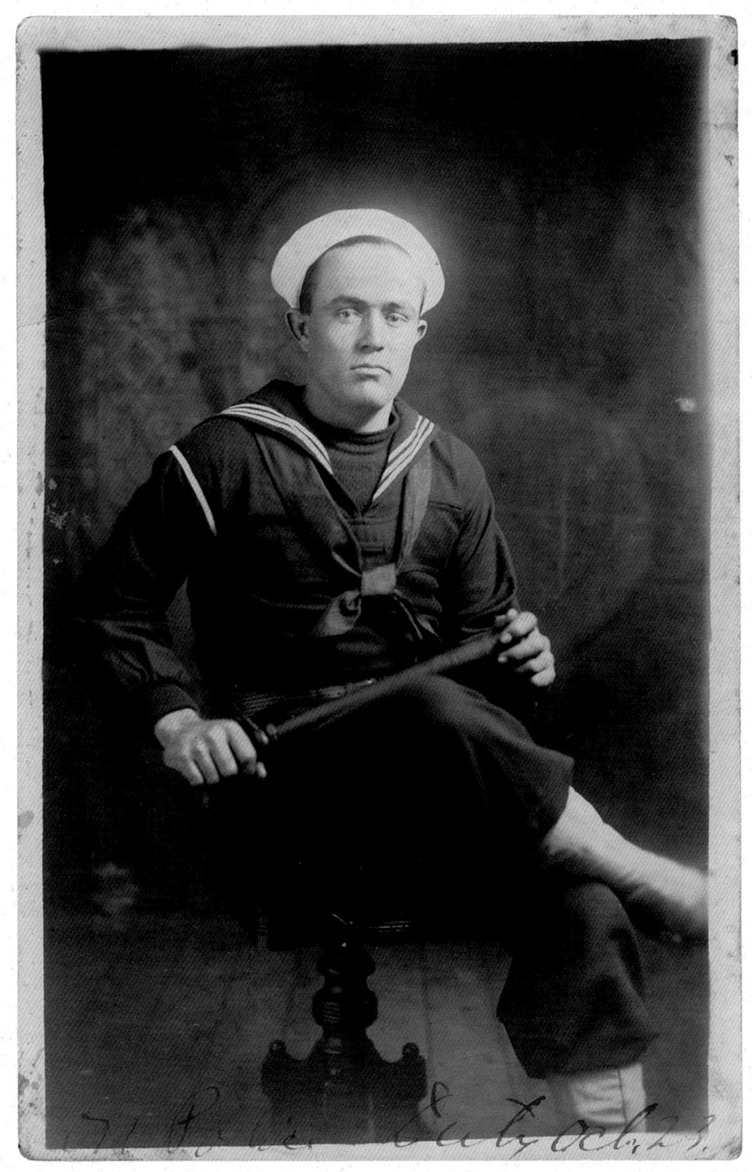

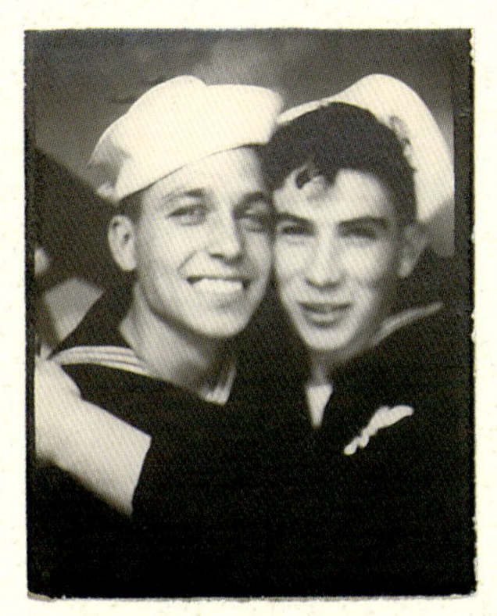

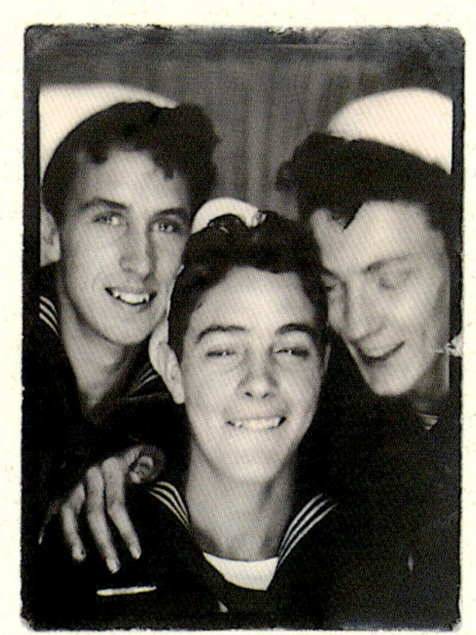

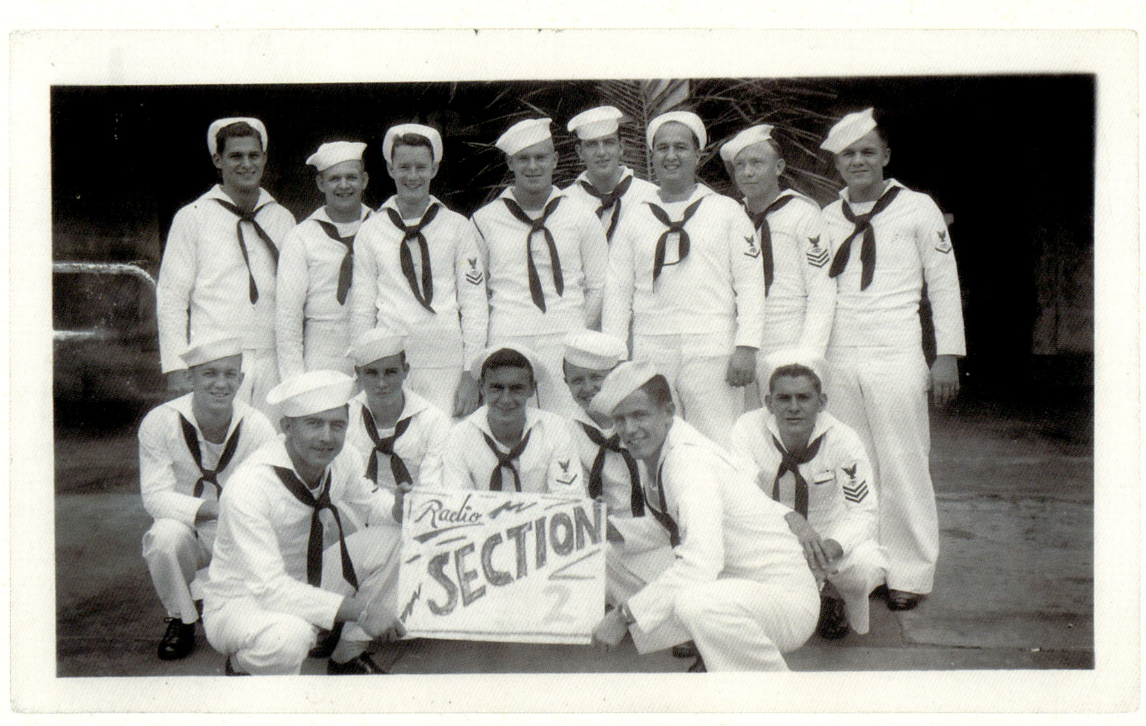
Radio
SECTION
2

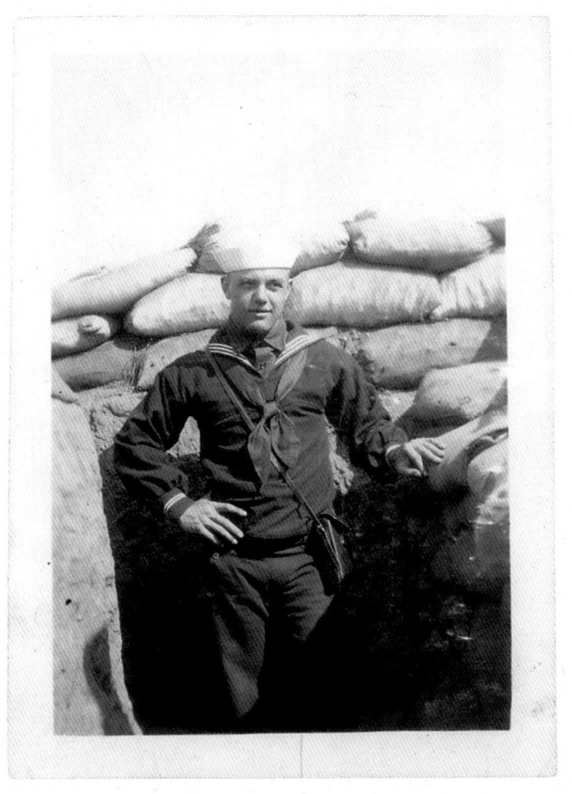

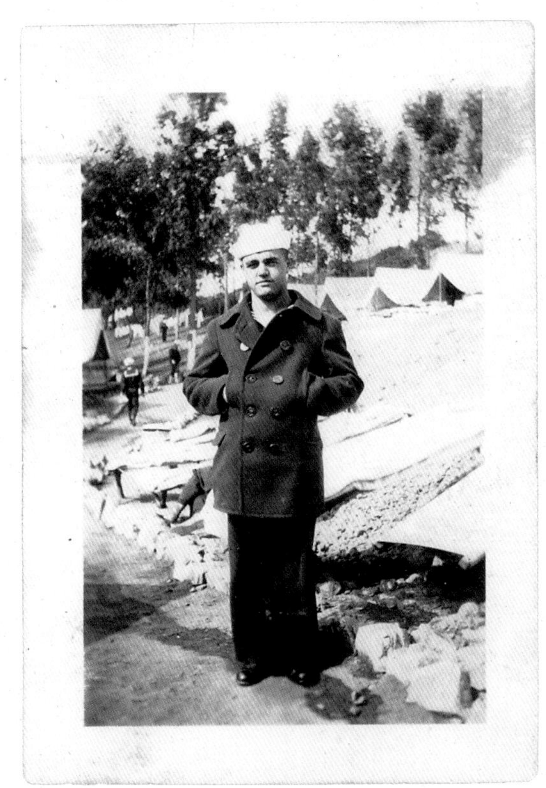

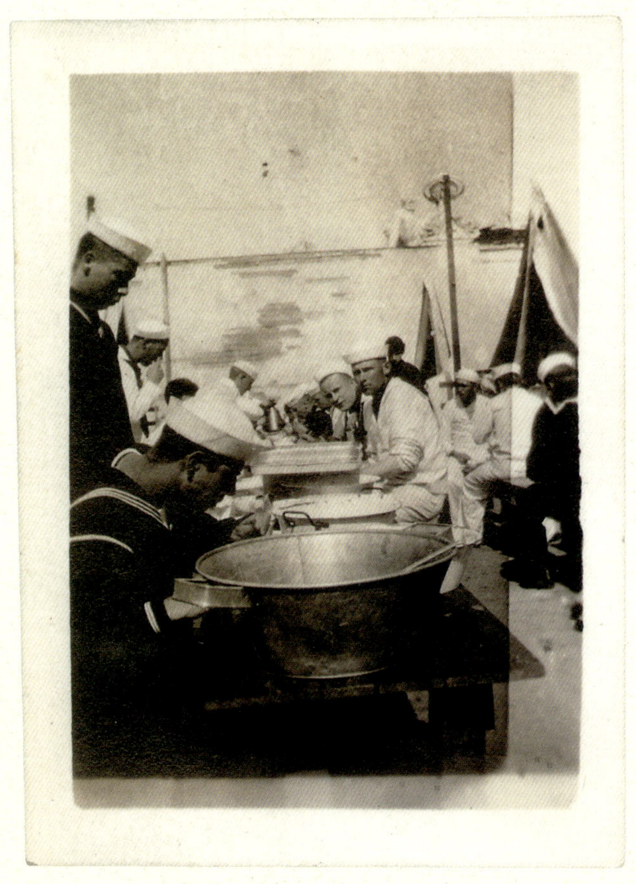

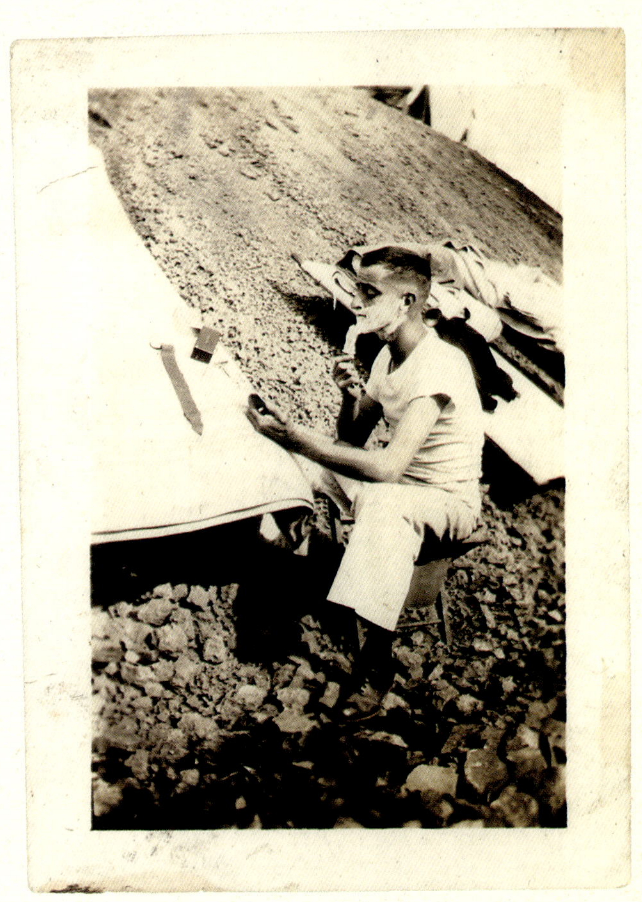

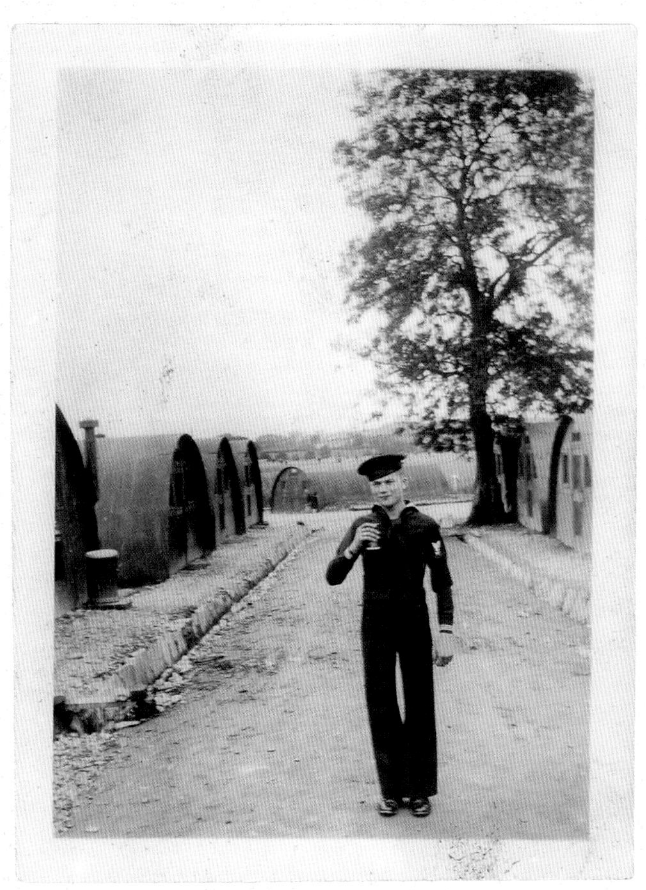

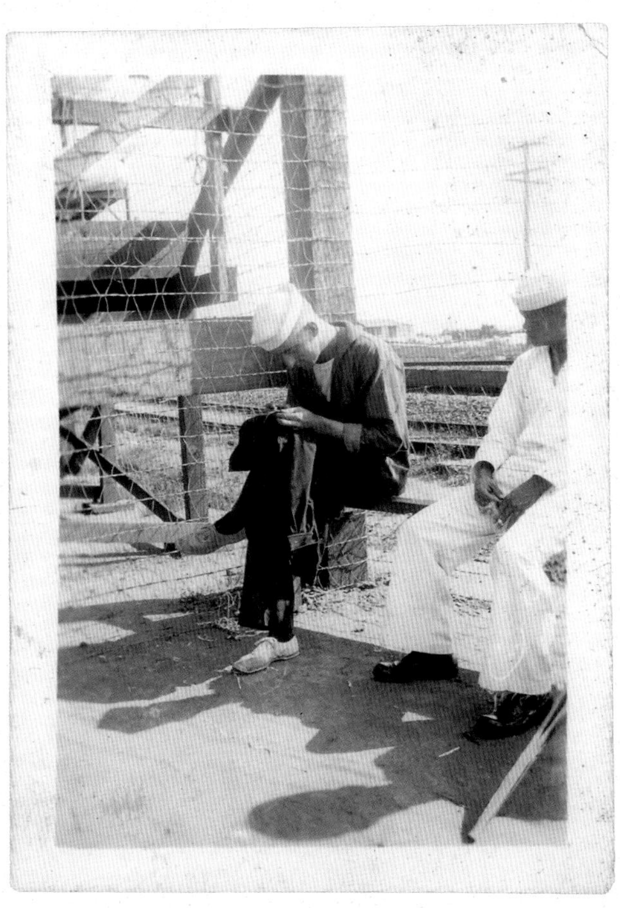

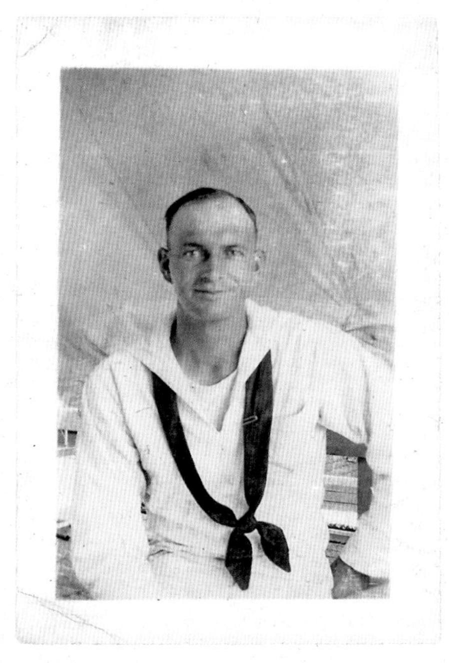

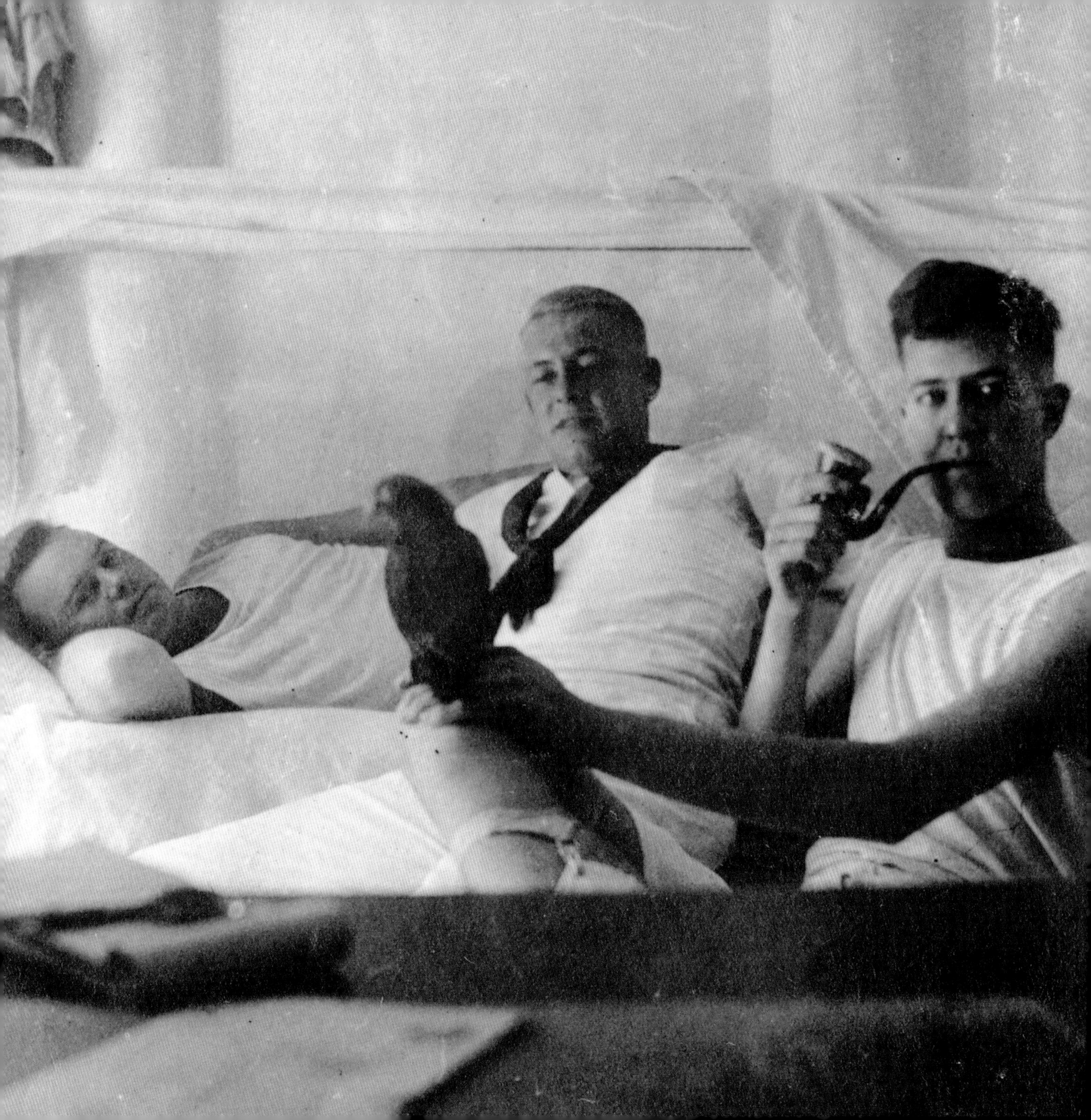

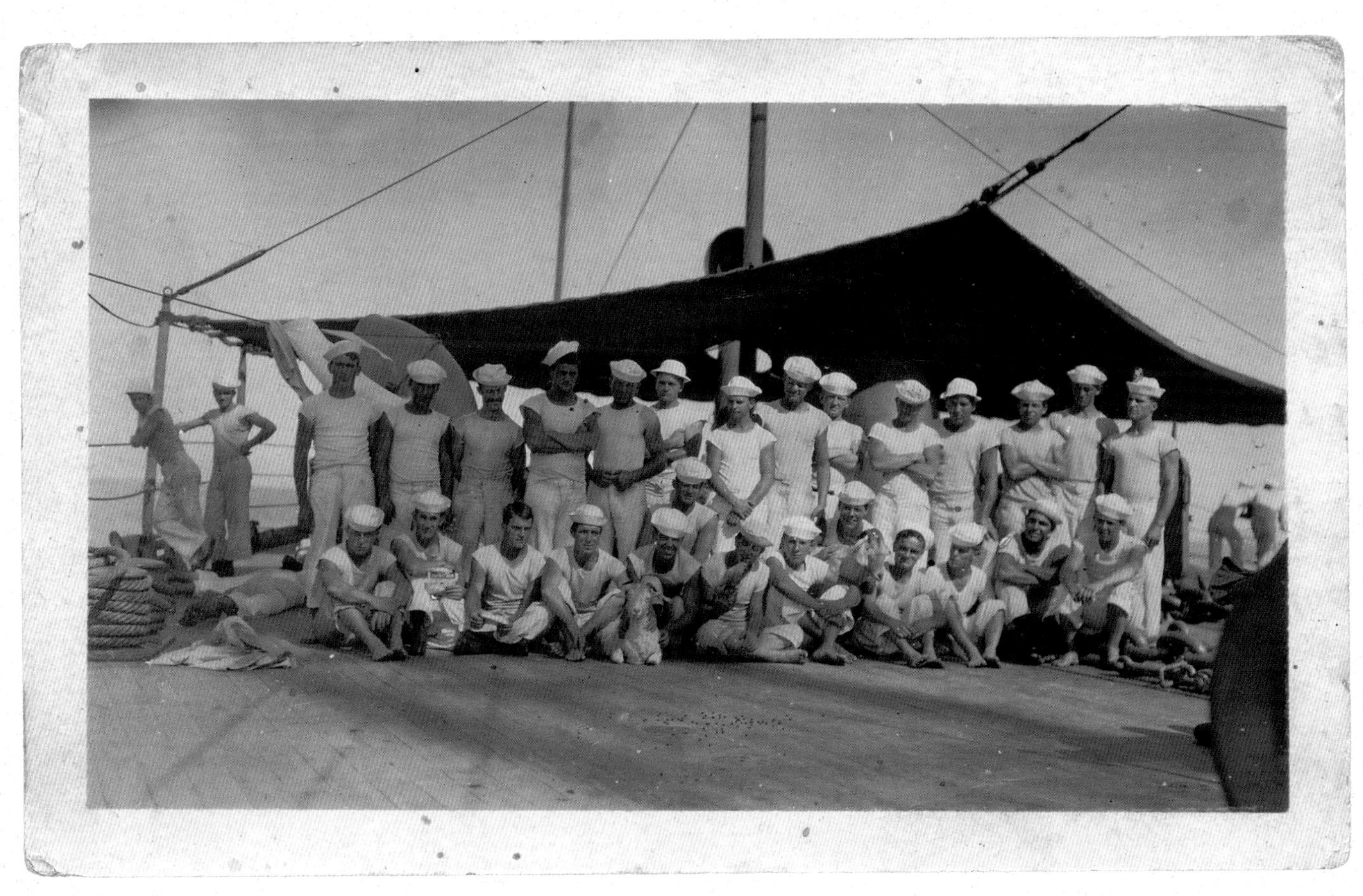

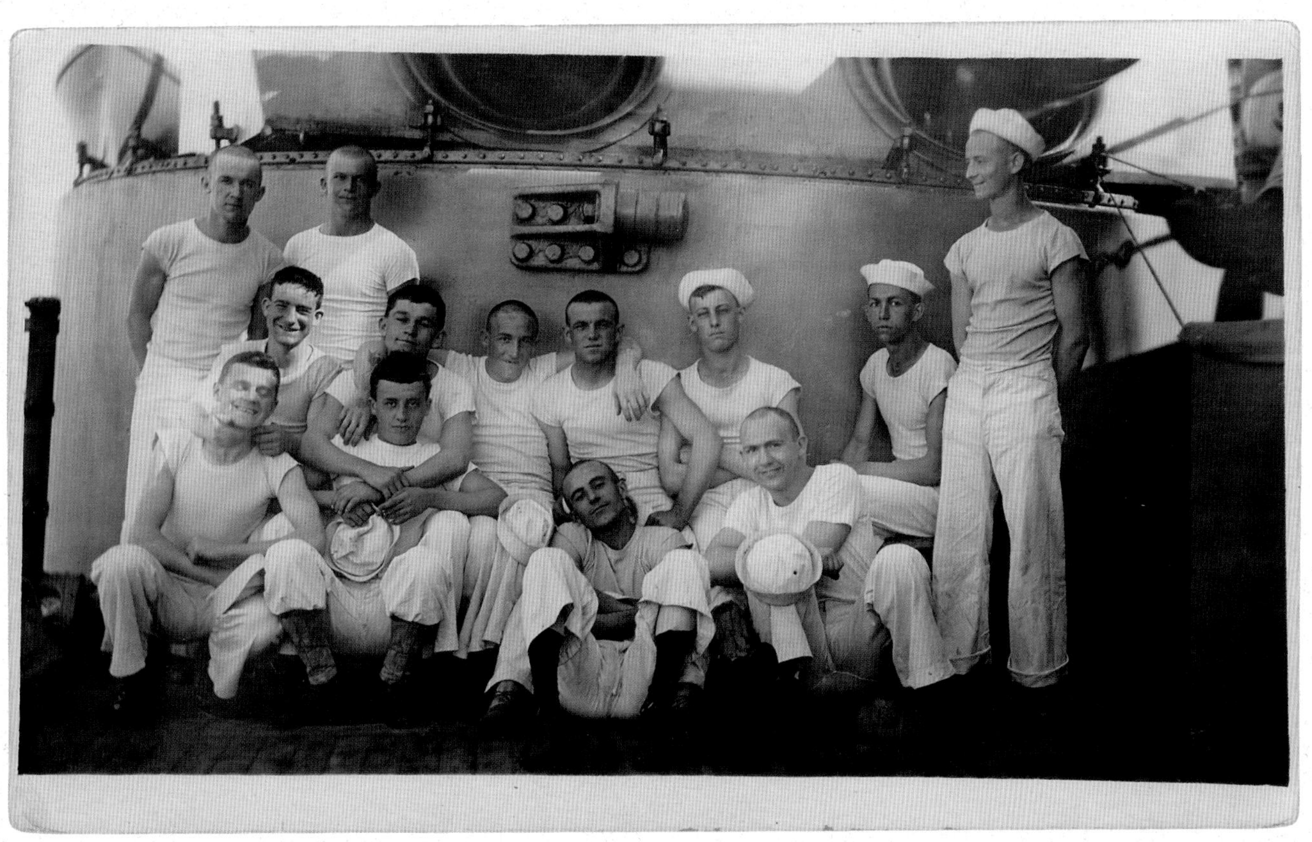

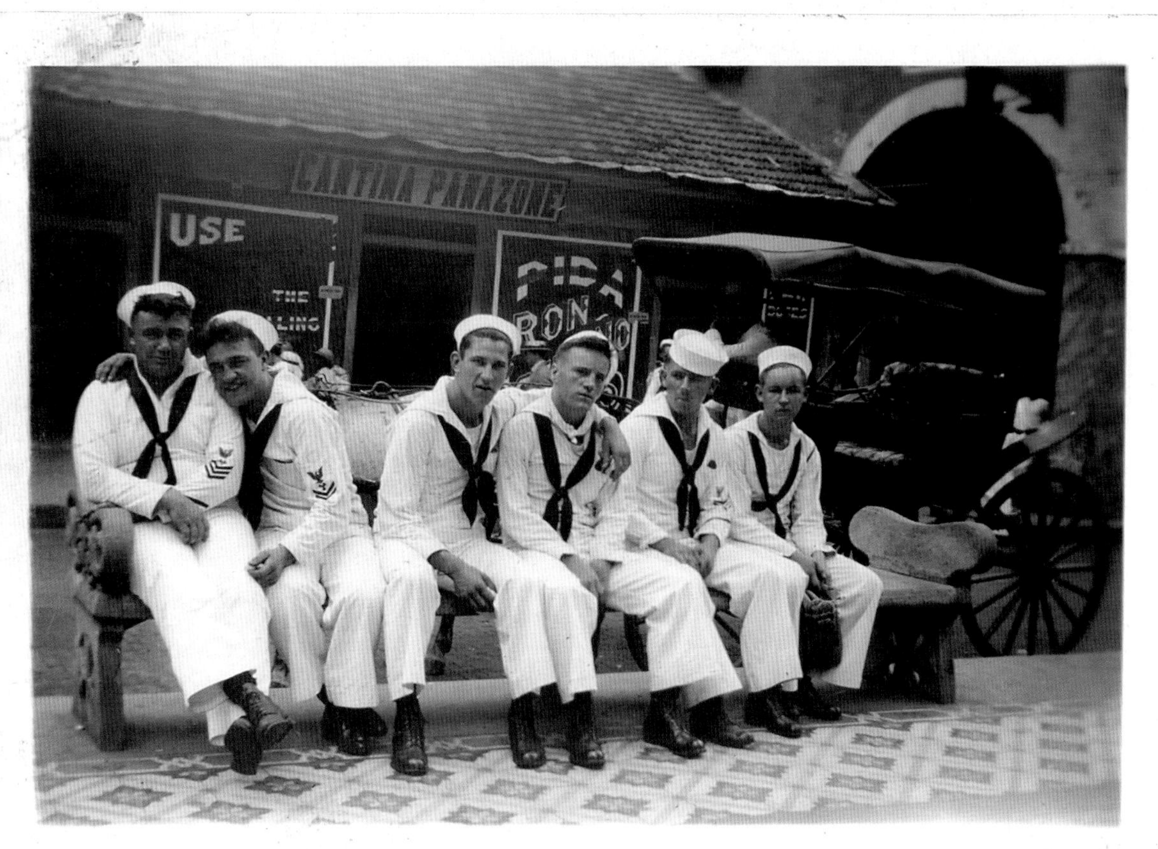
CANTINA PANAZONE
USE
THE
PIDA
RON

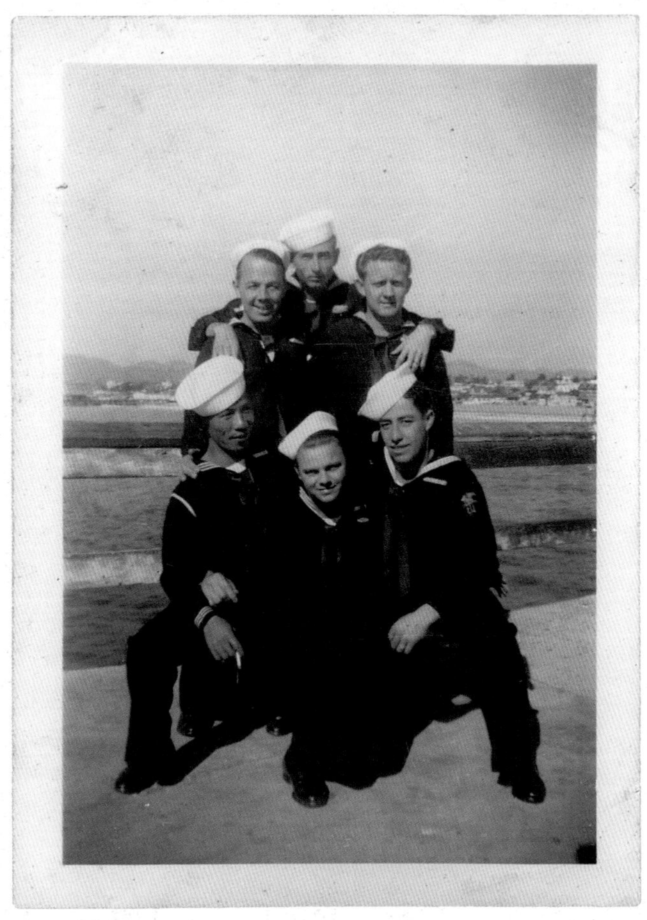

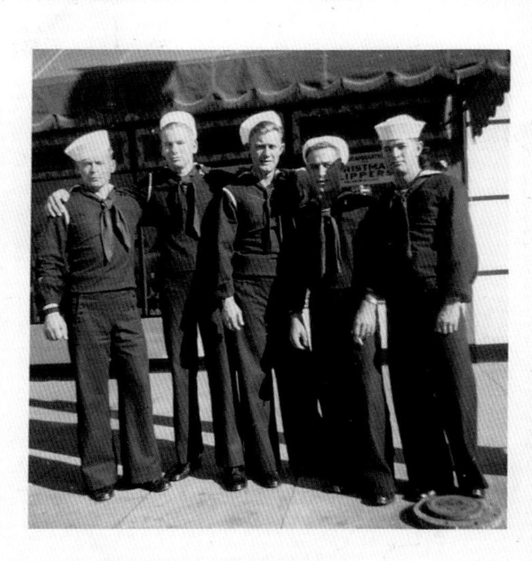

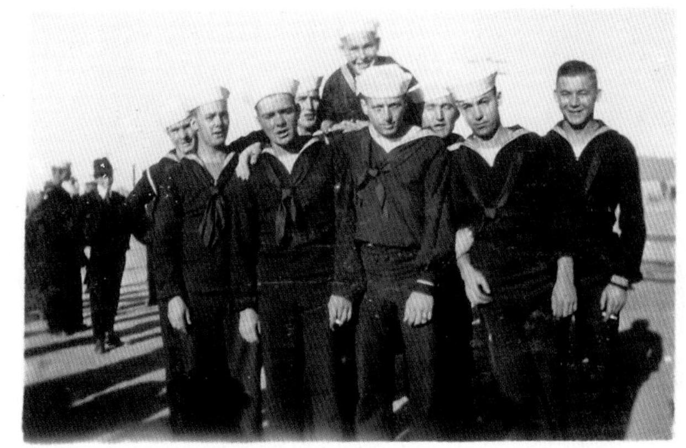

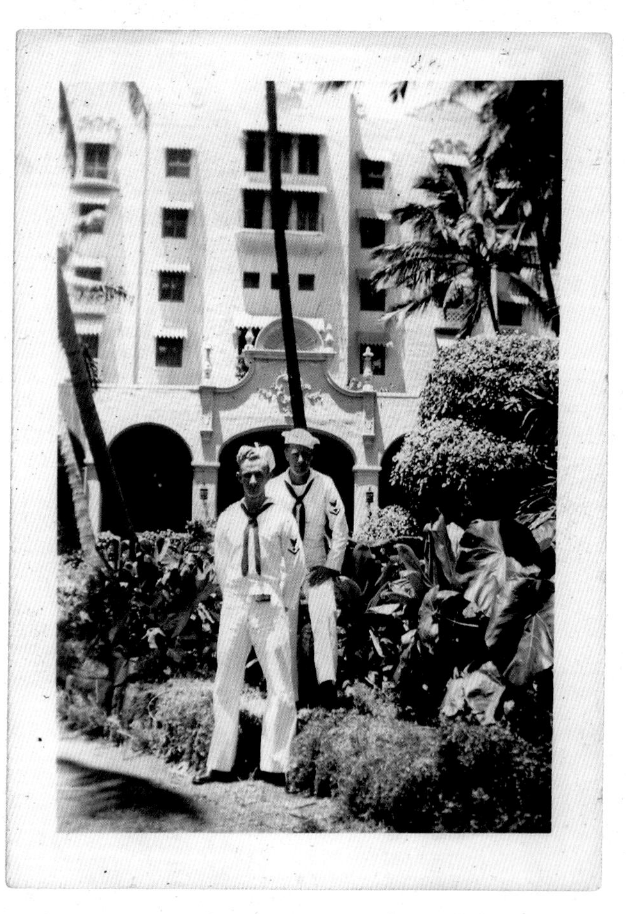

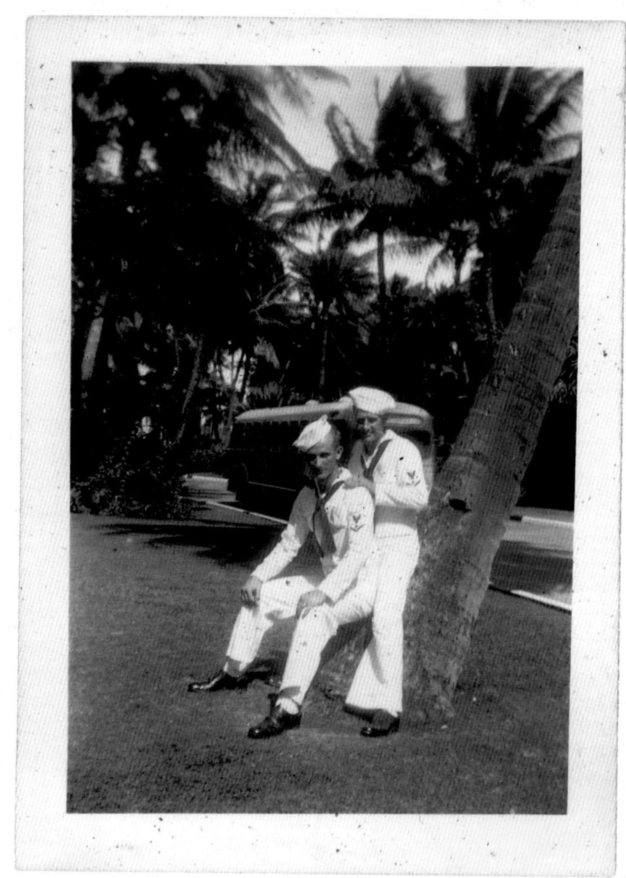

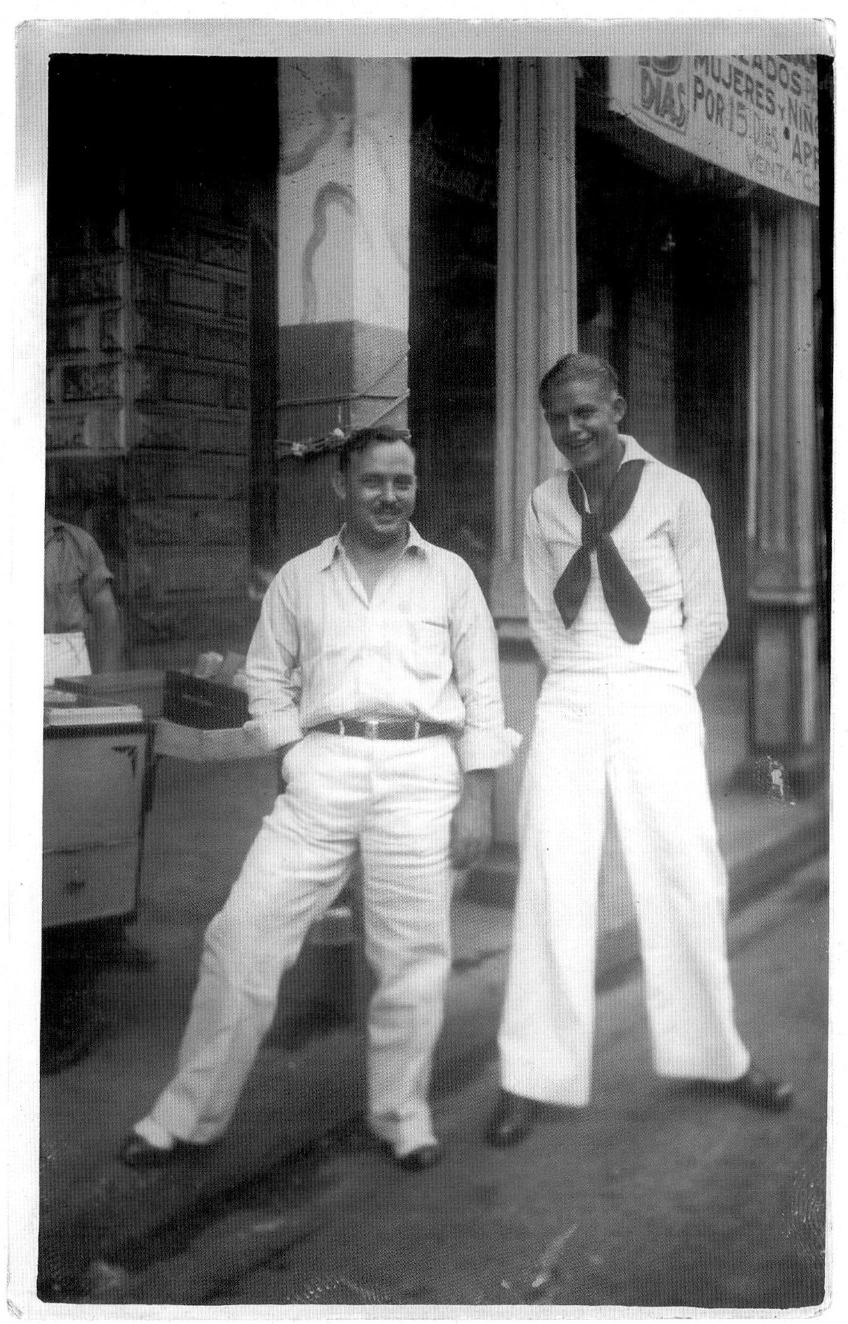
DIAS
MUJERES y
POR 15 DIAS

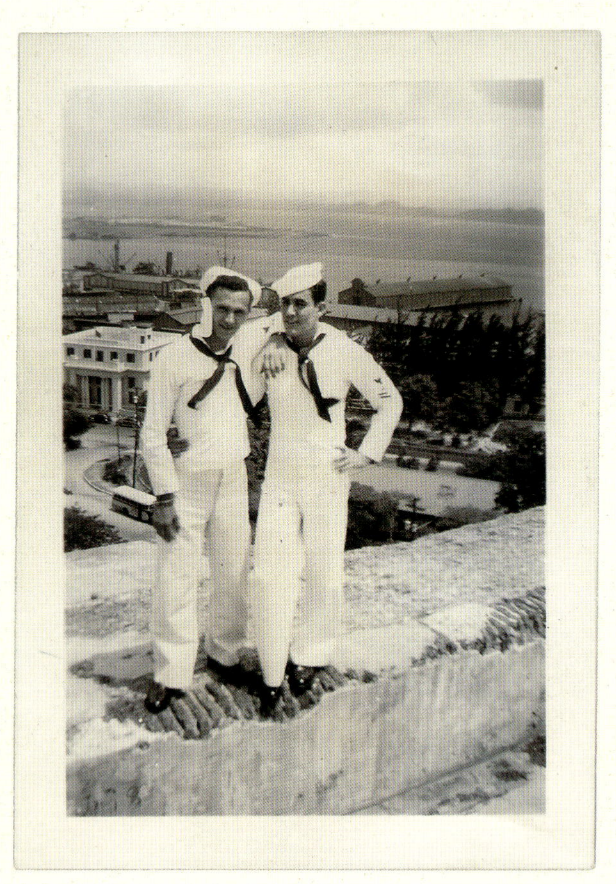

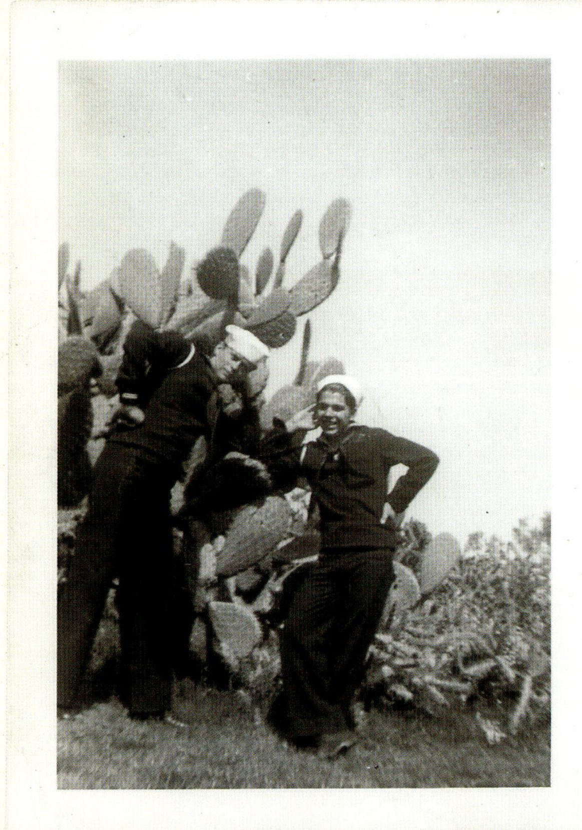

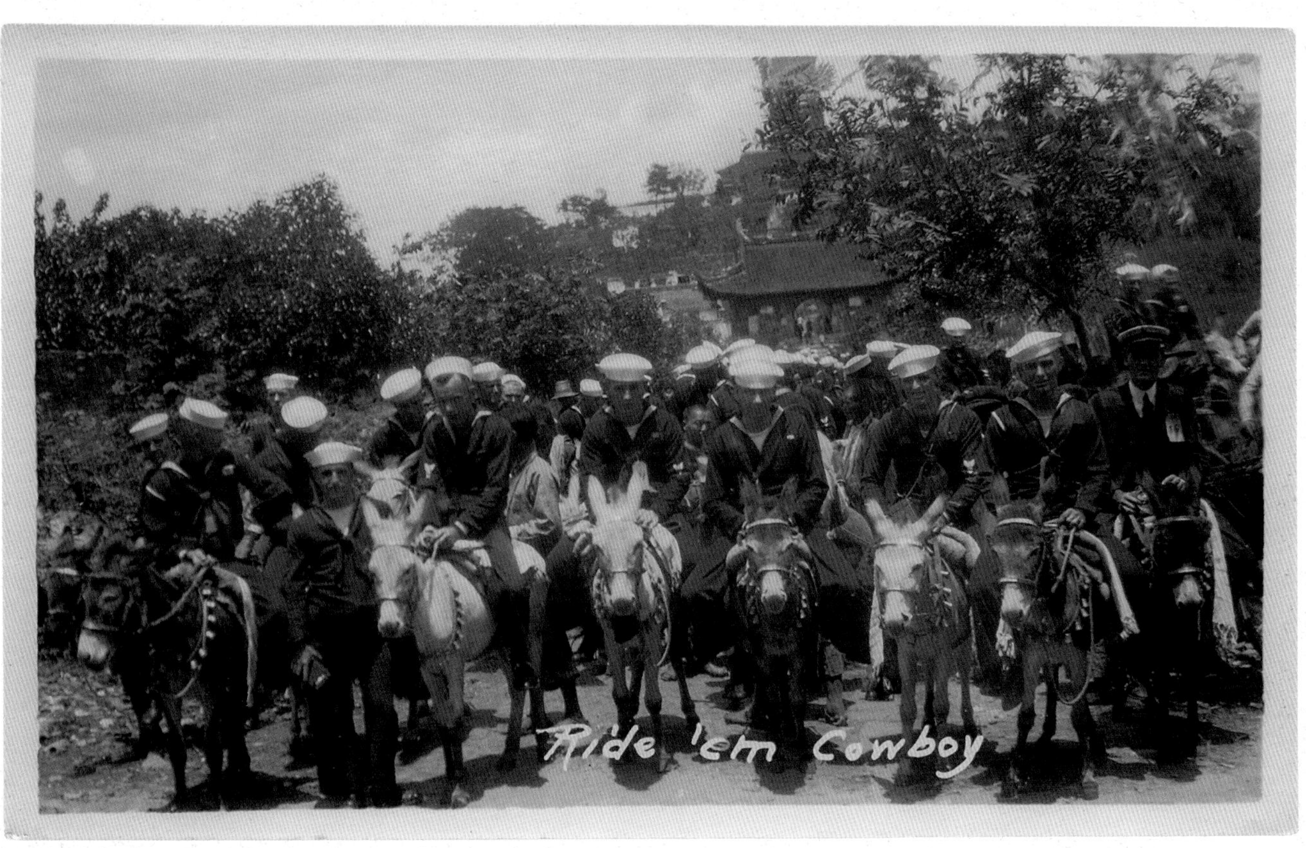
Ride 'em Cowboy

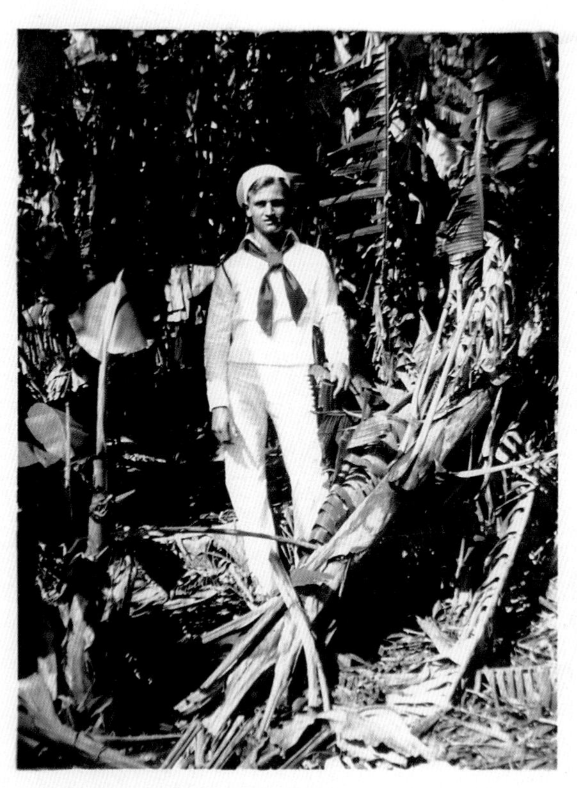

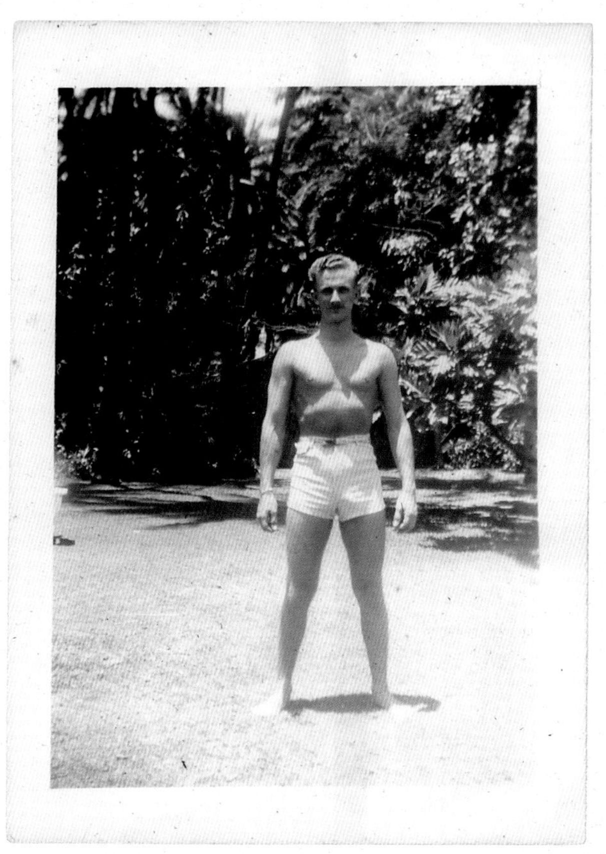

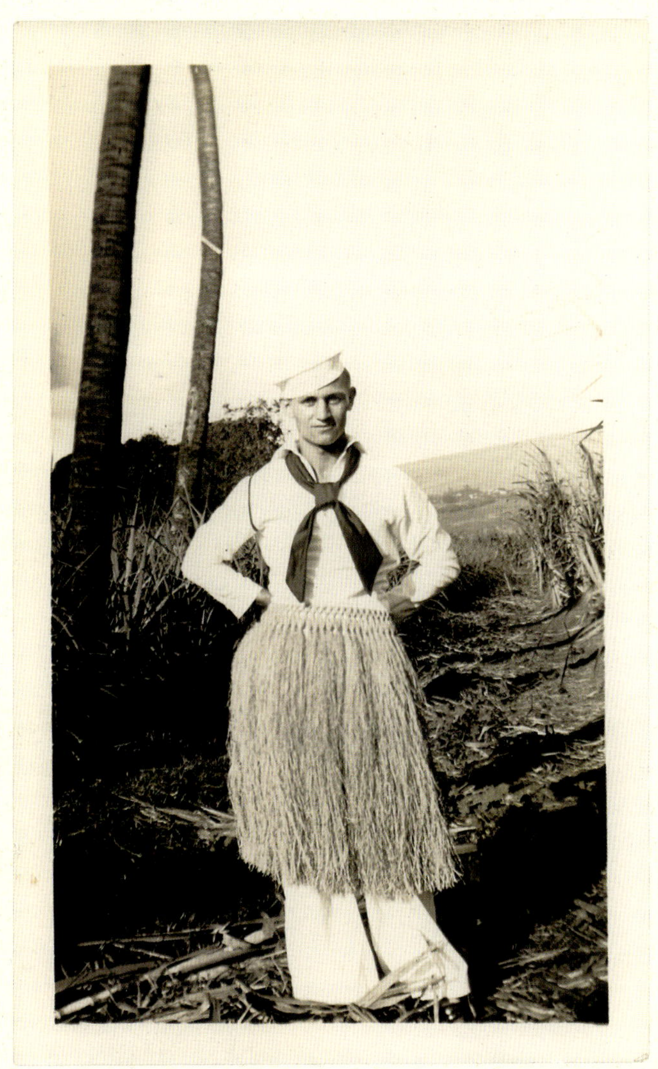

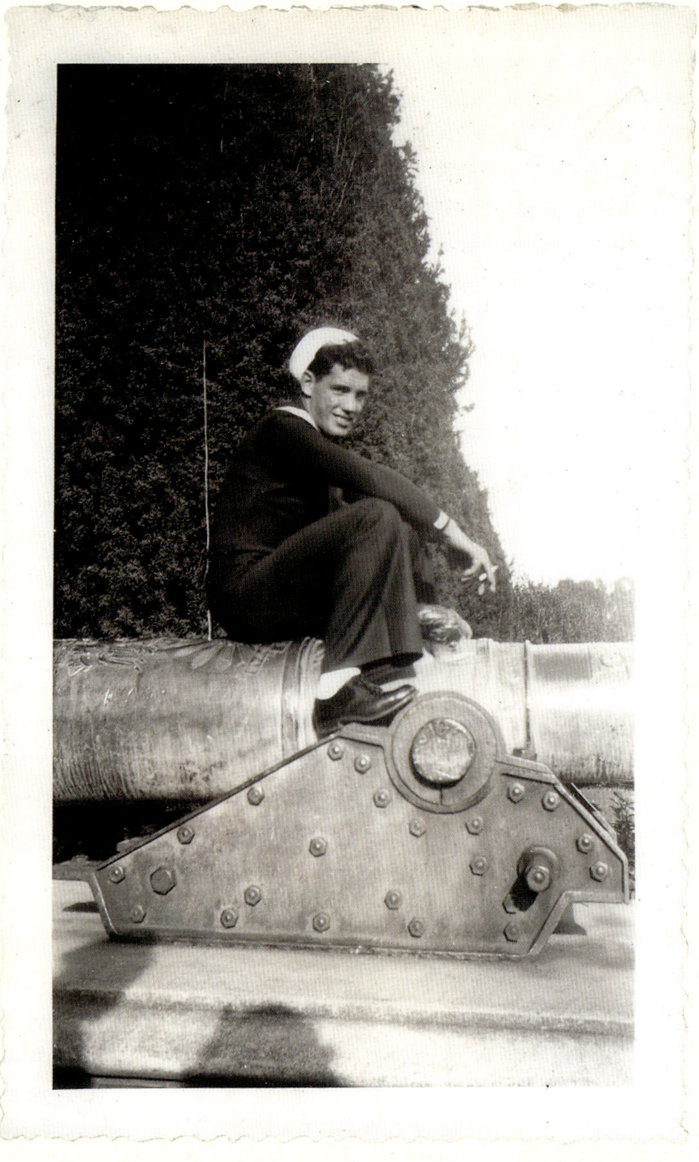

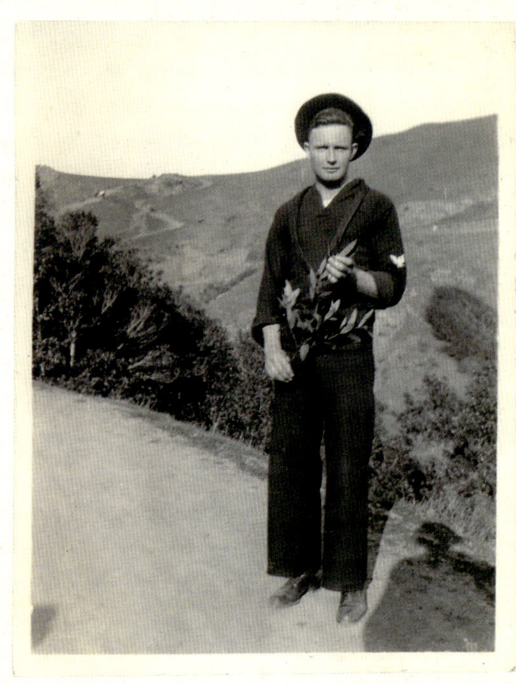

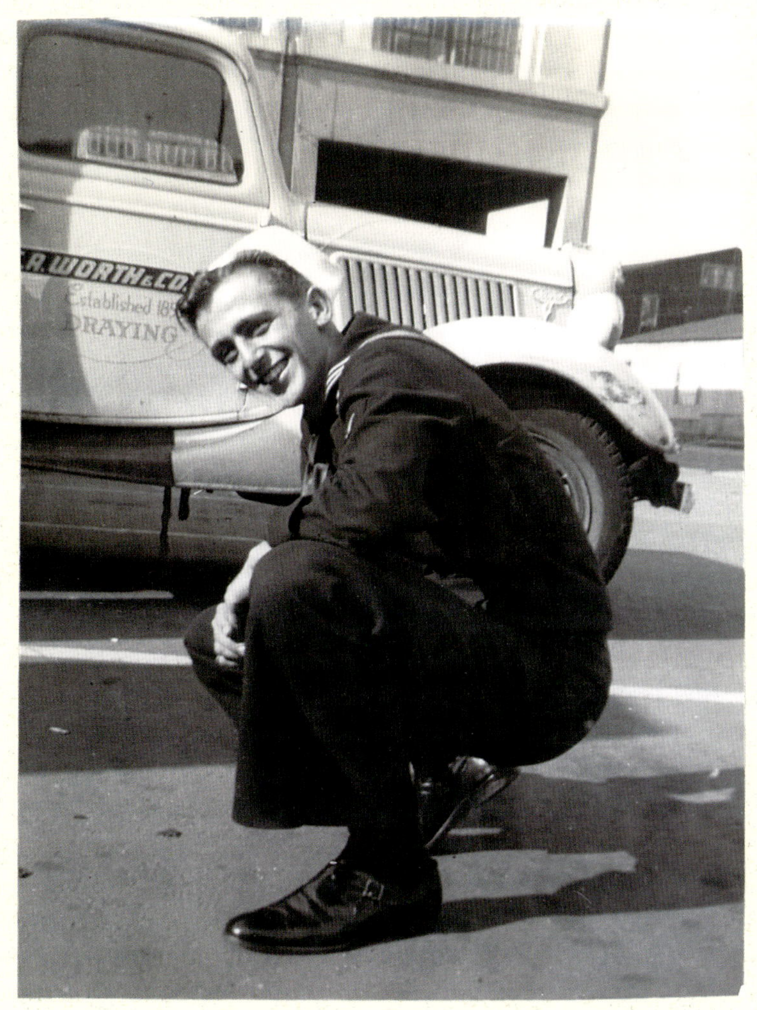
WORTH & CO.
DRAYING

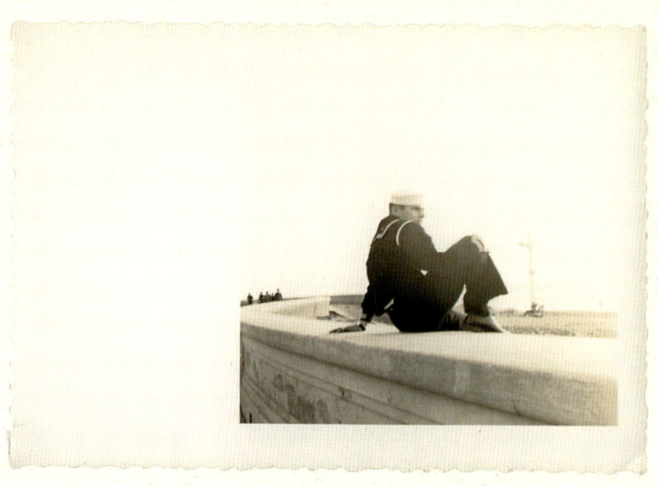

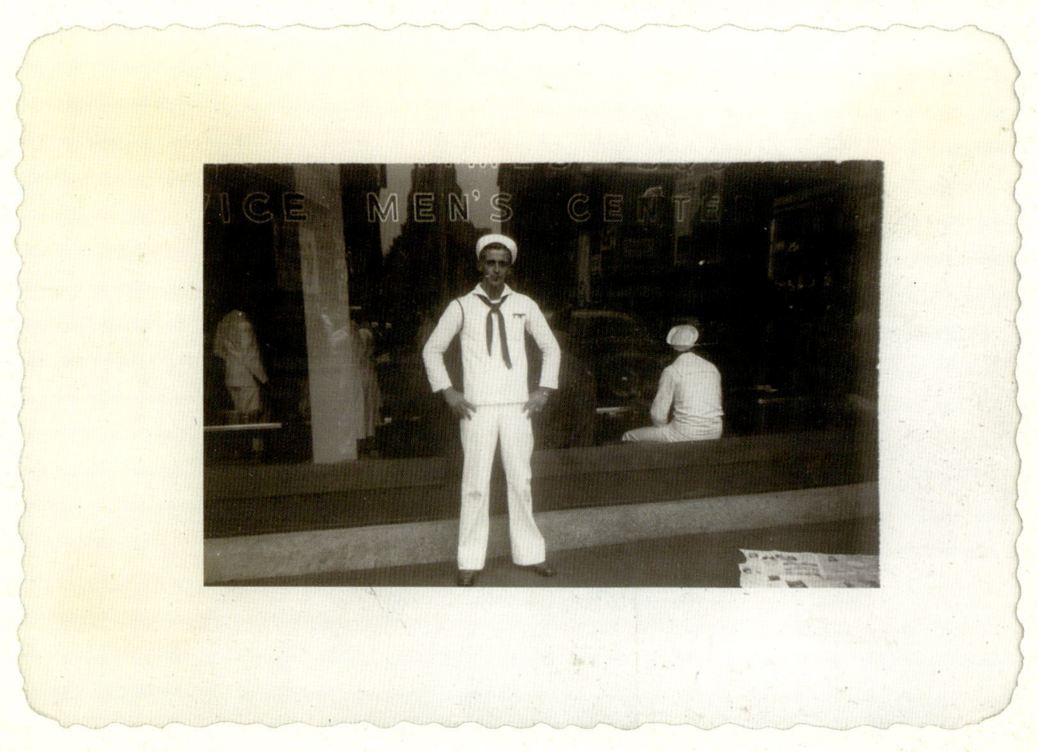
VICE MEN'S CENTE

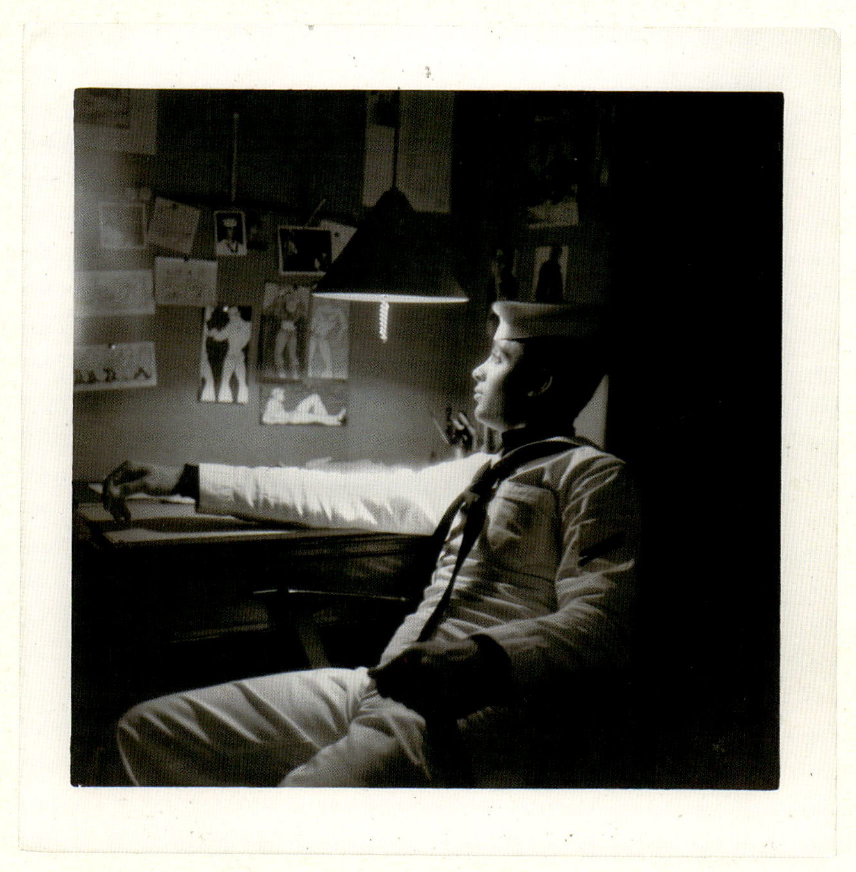

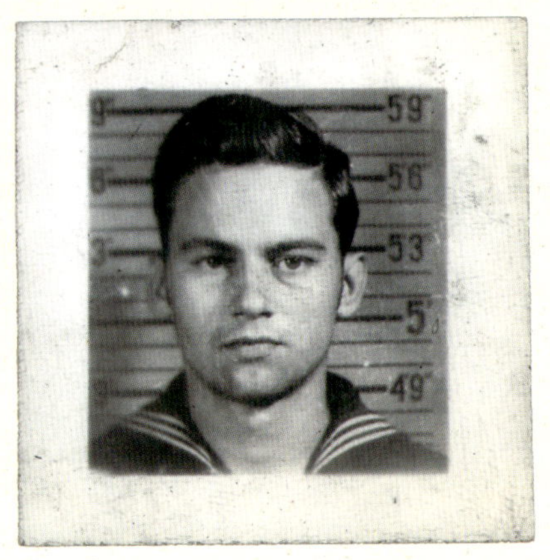
59
56
53
49

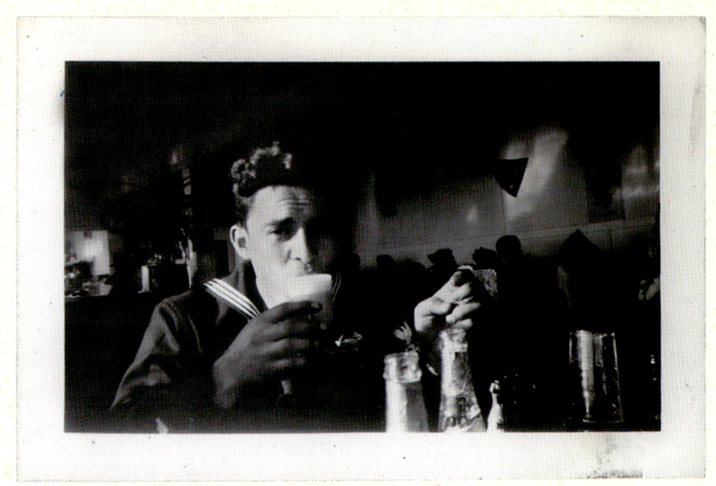

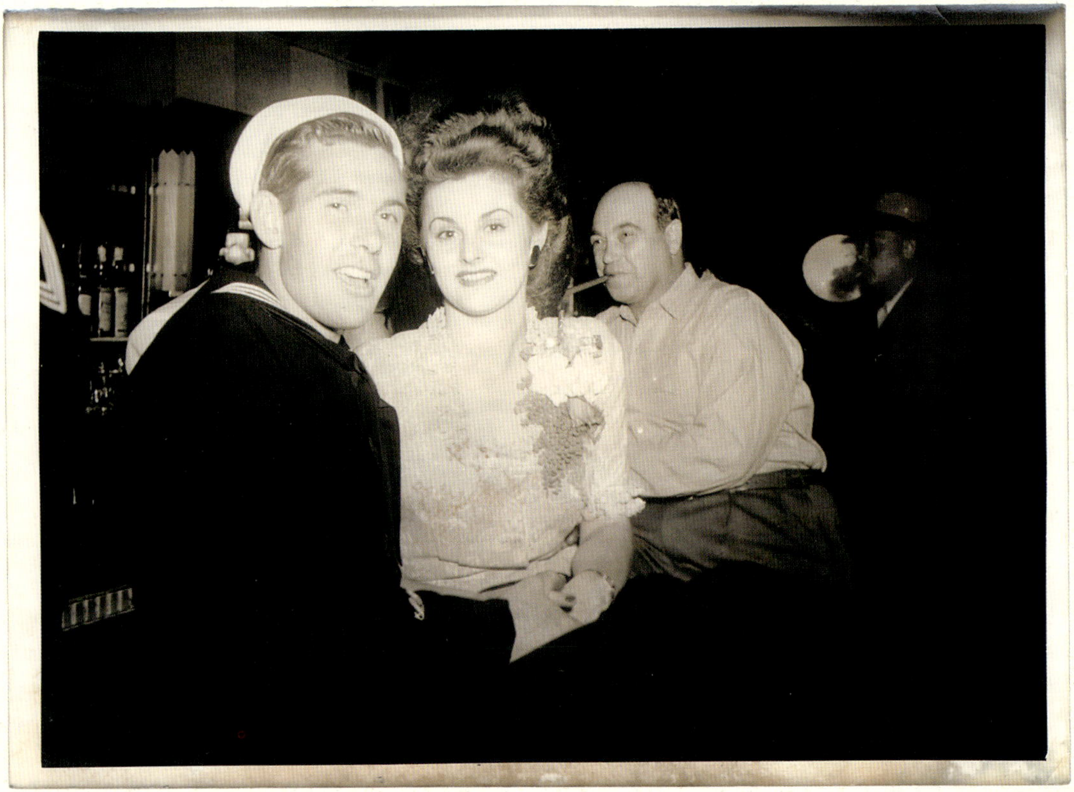

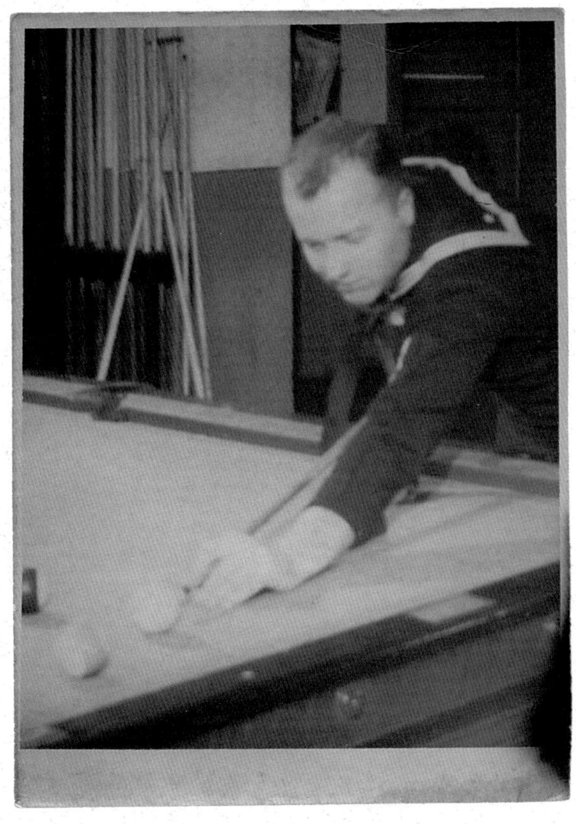

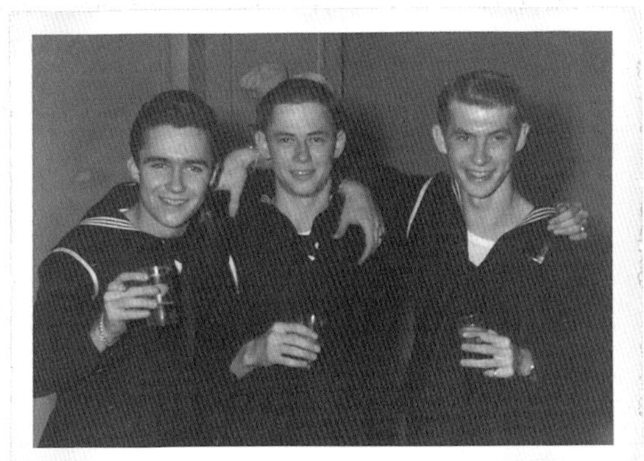

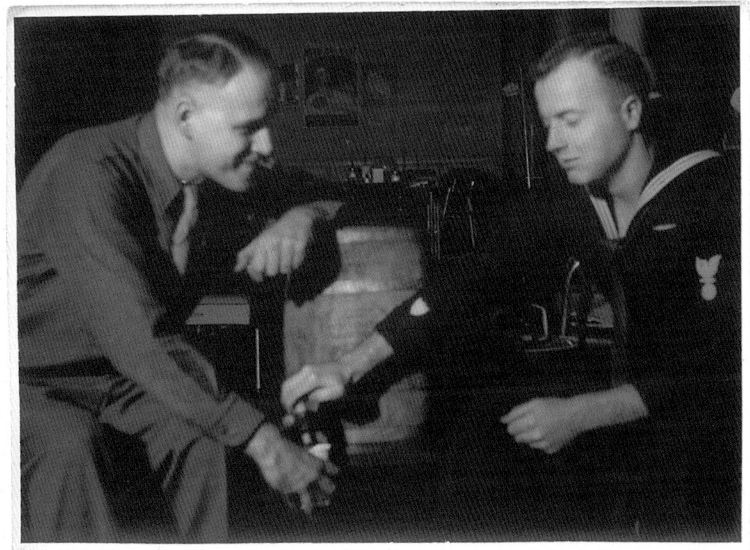

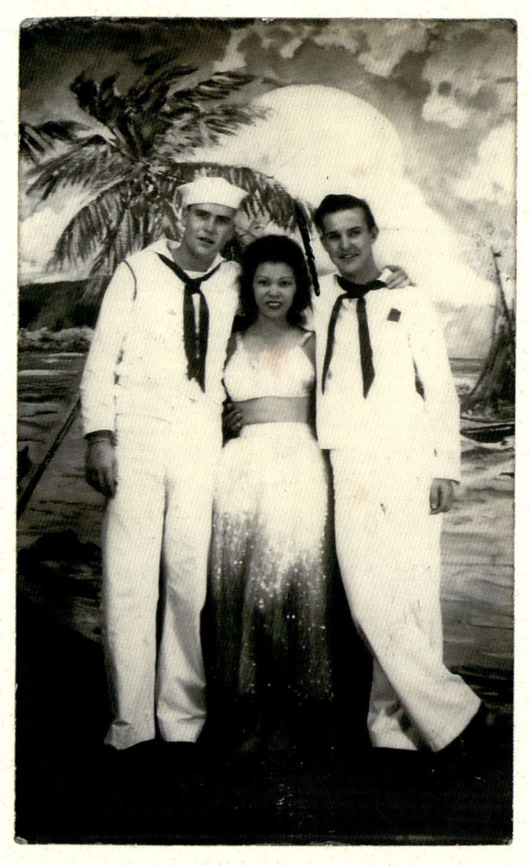

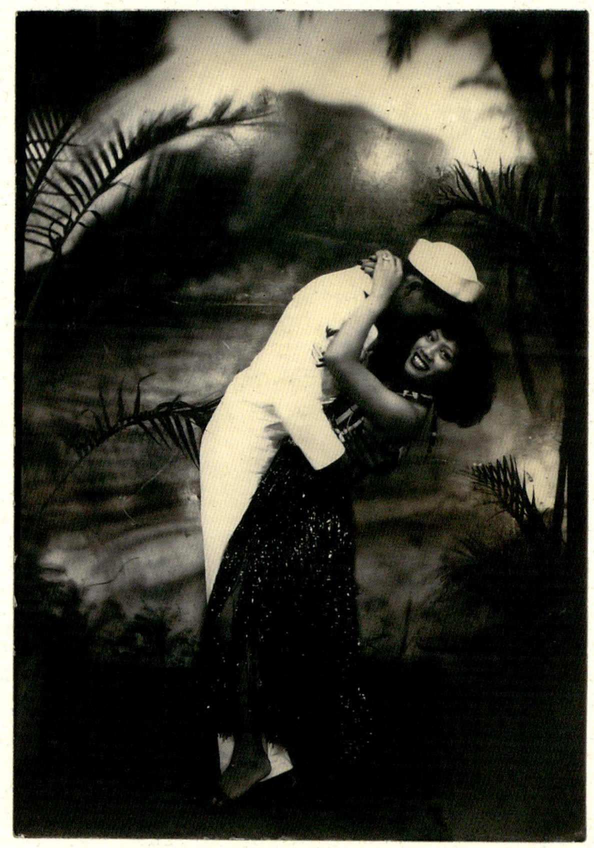

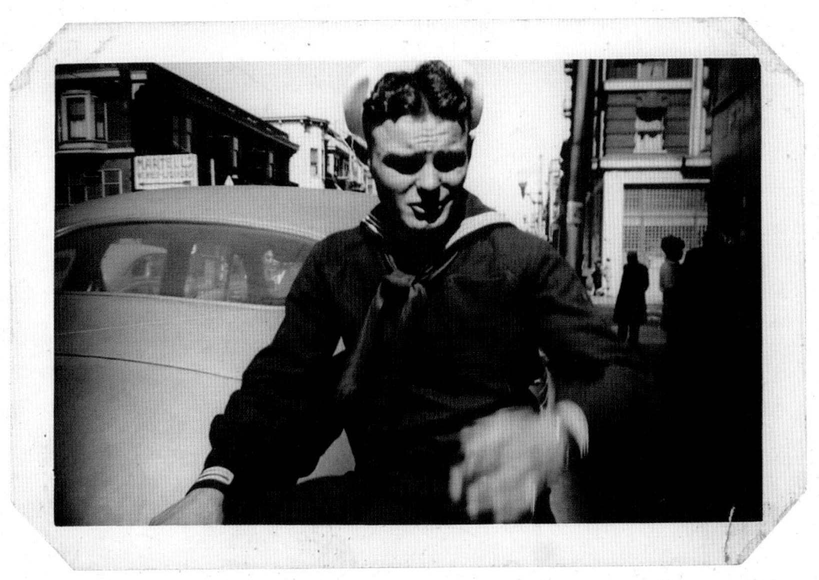

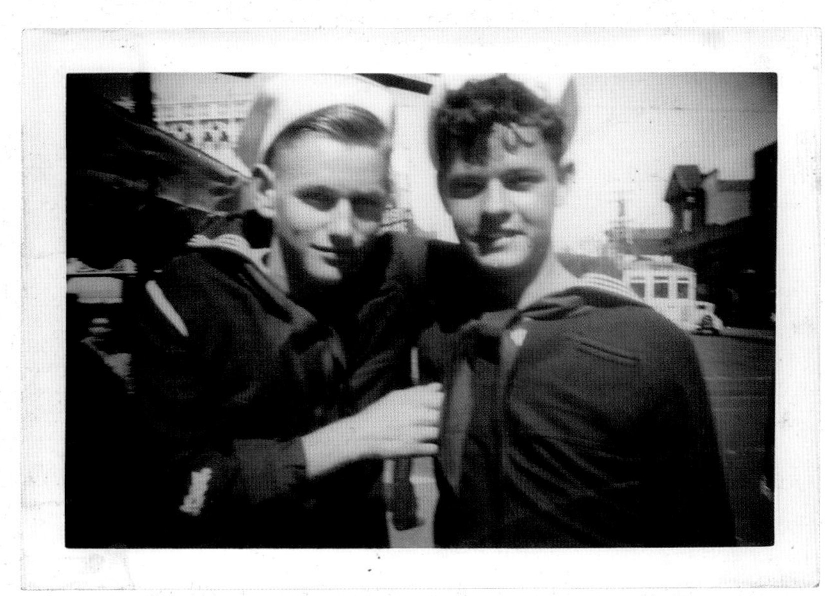

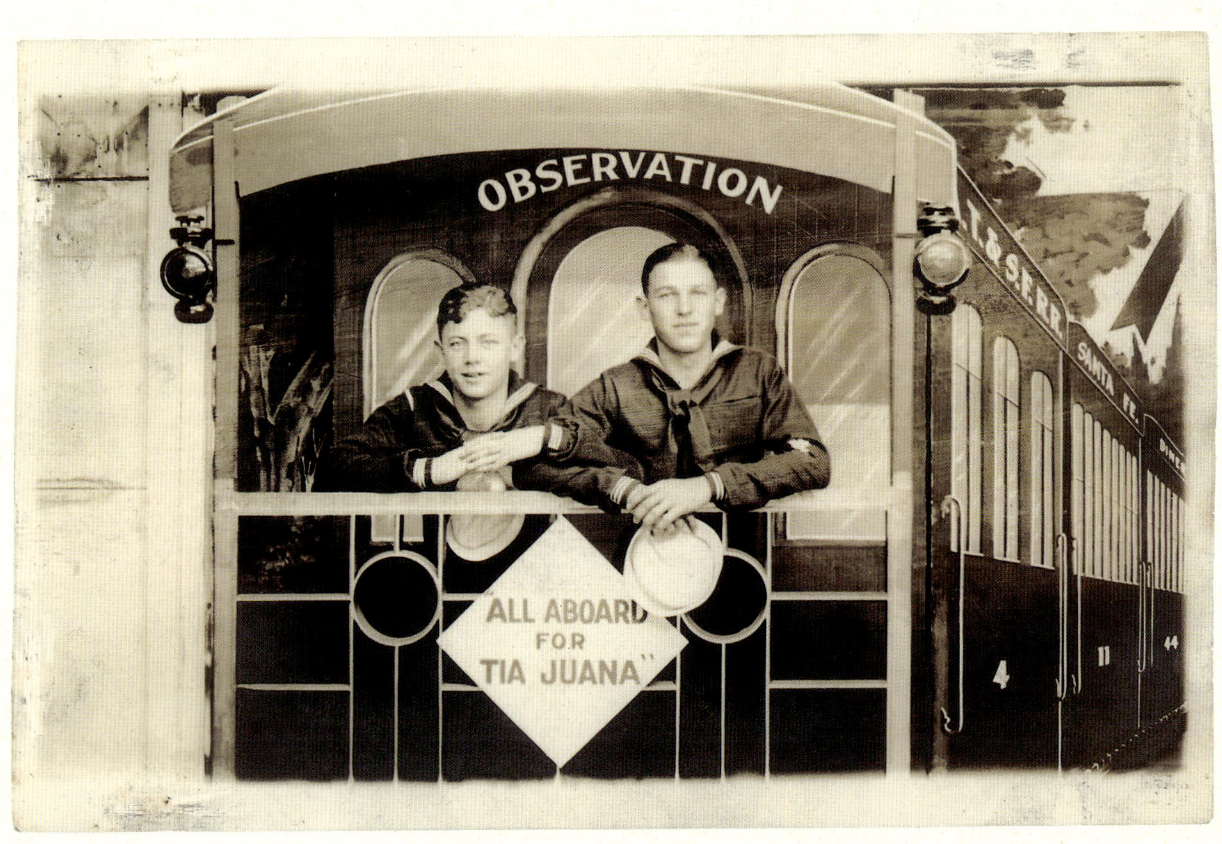
OBSERVATION
T.&S.F.R.R.
SANTA FE.
ALL ABOARD
FOR
TIA JUANA"
4
11
44

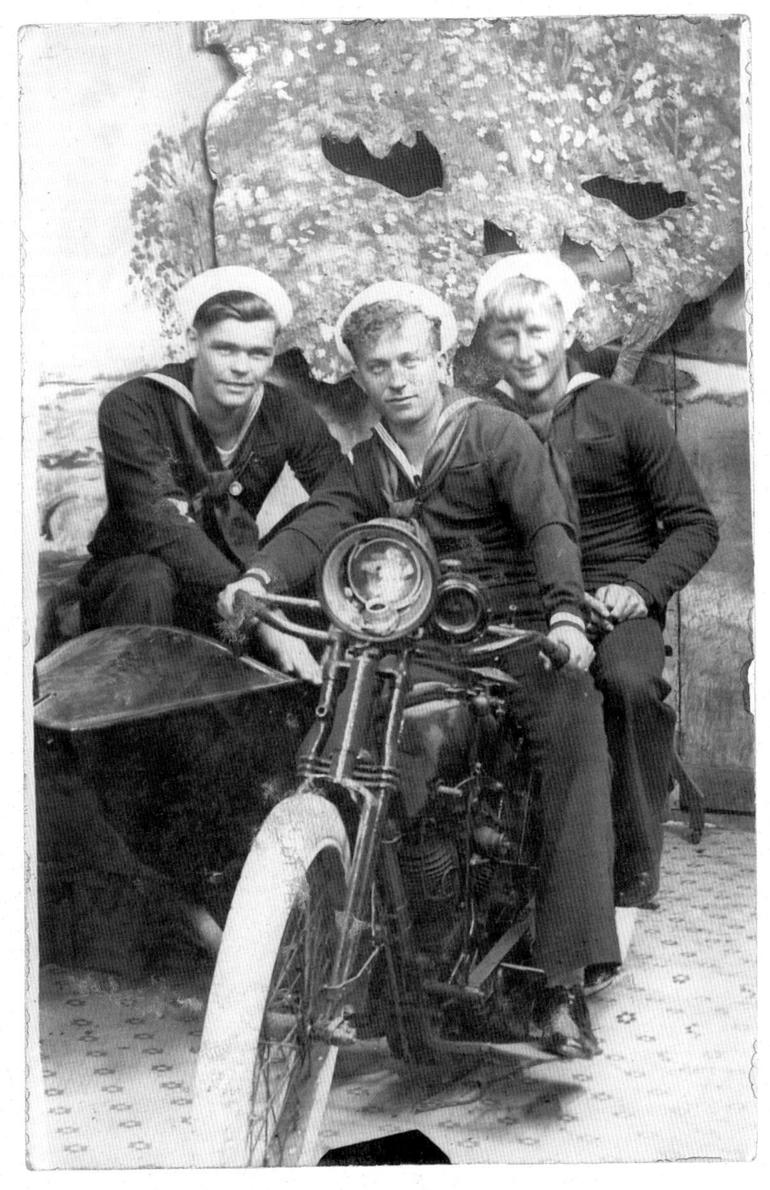

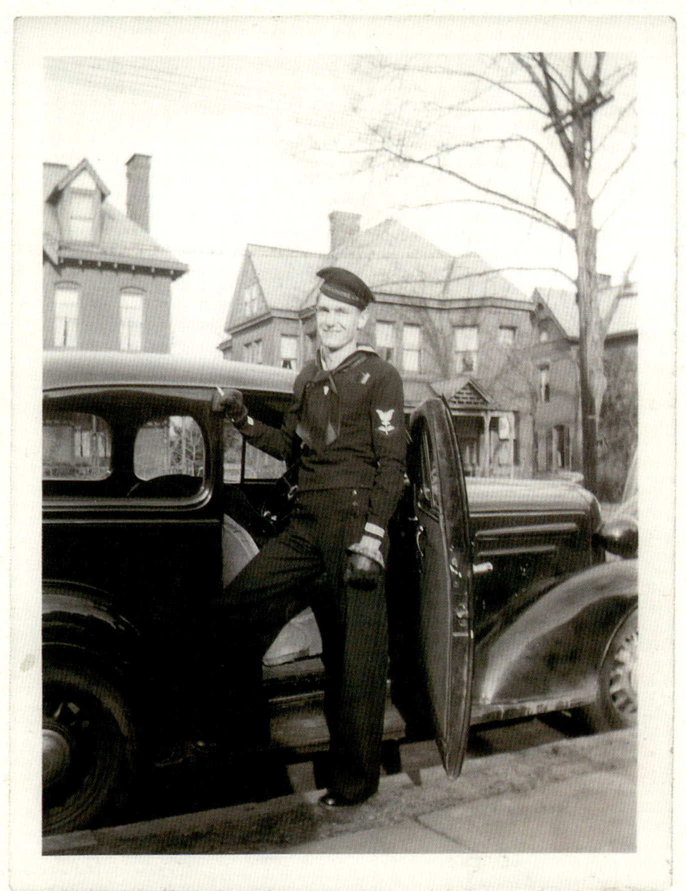

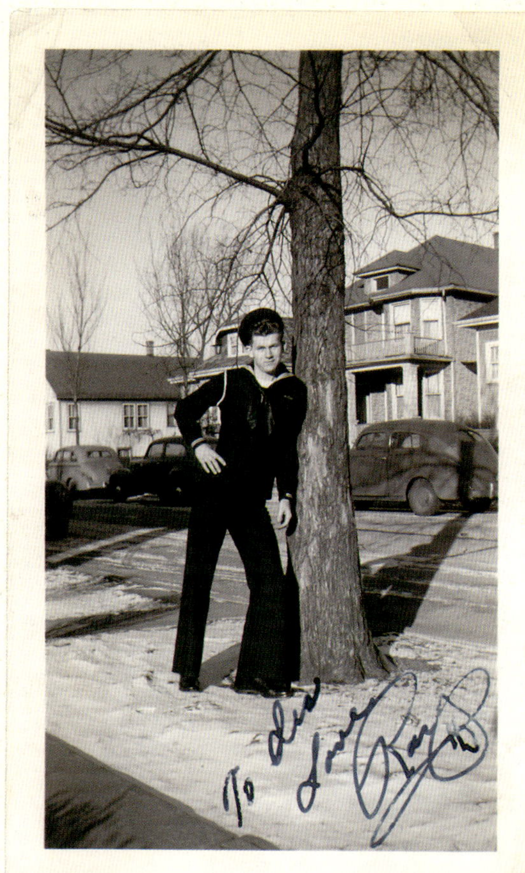

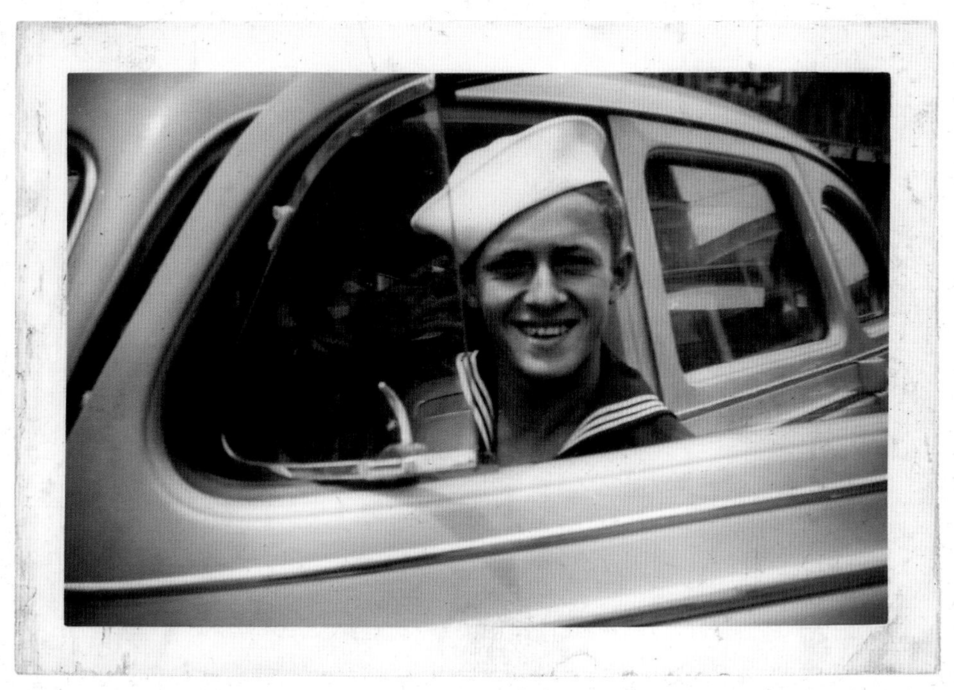

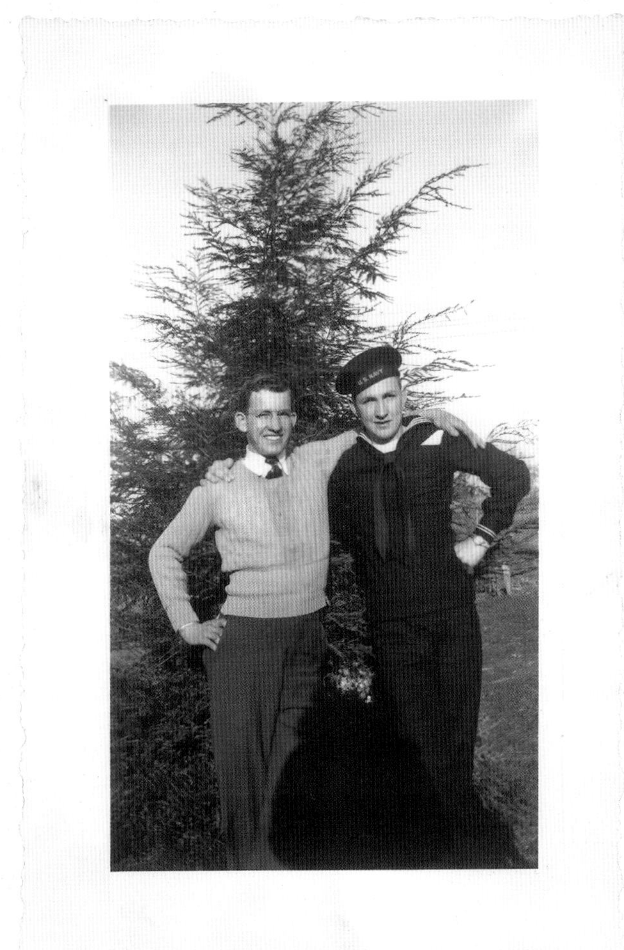

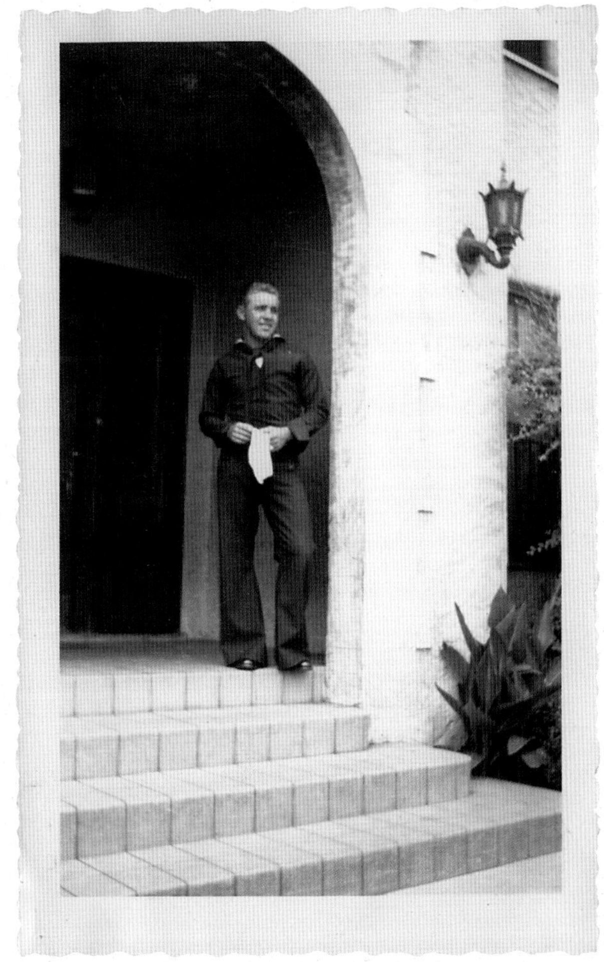

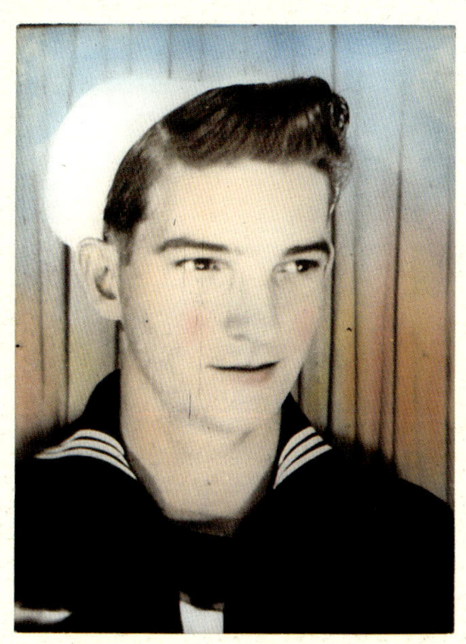

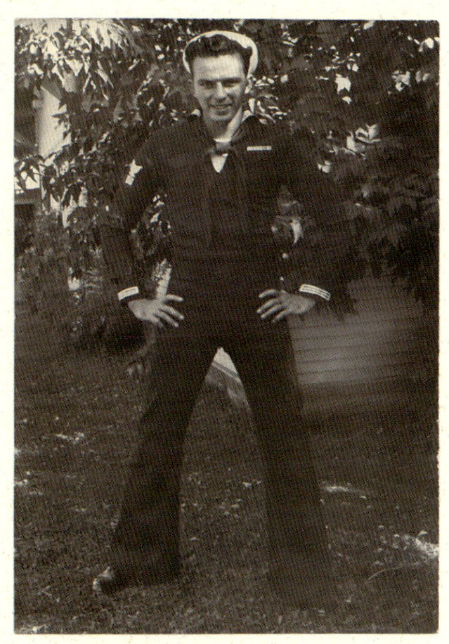

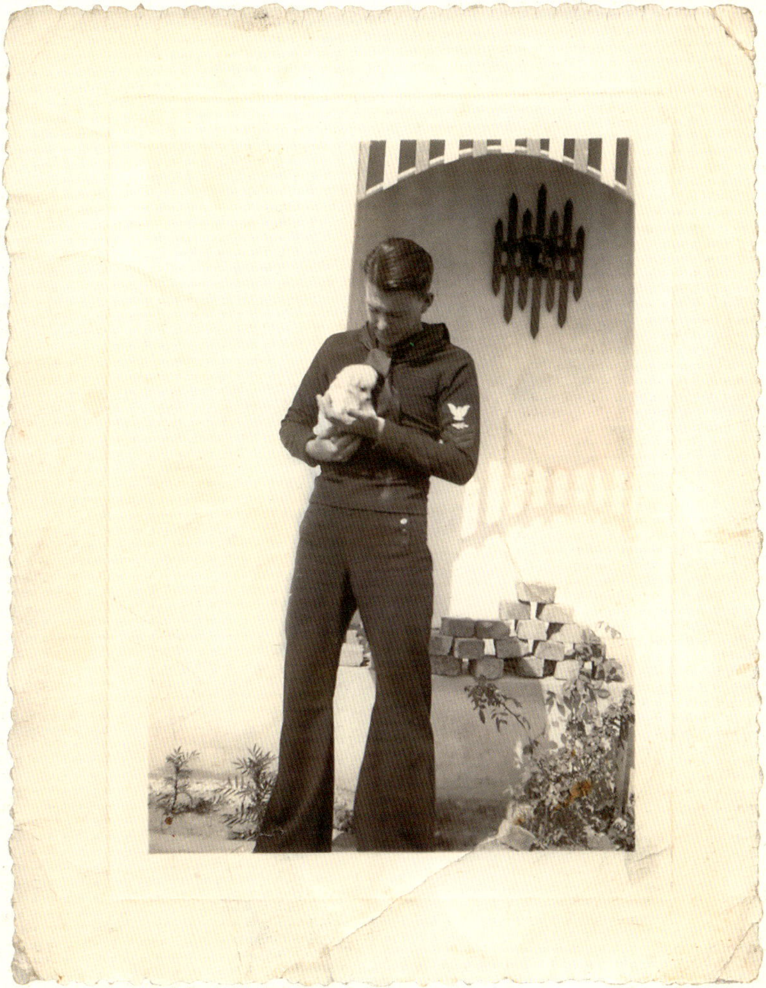

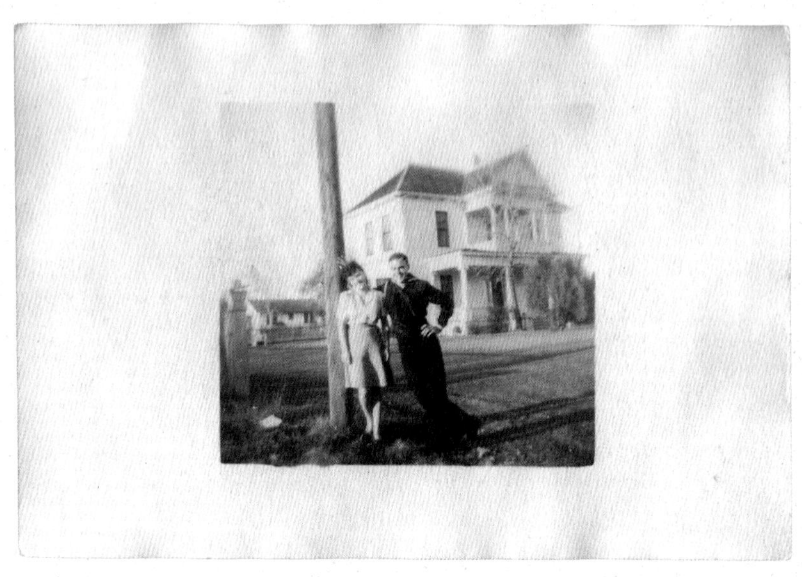

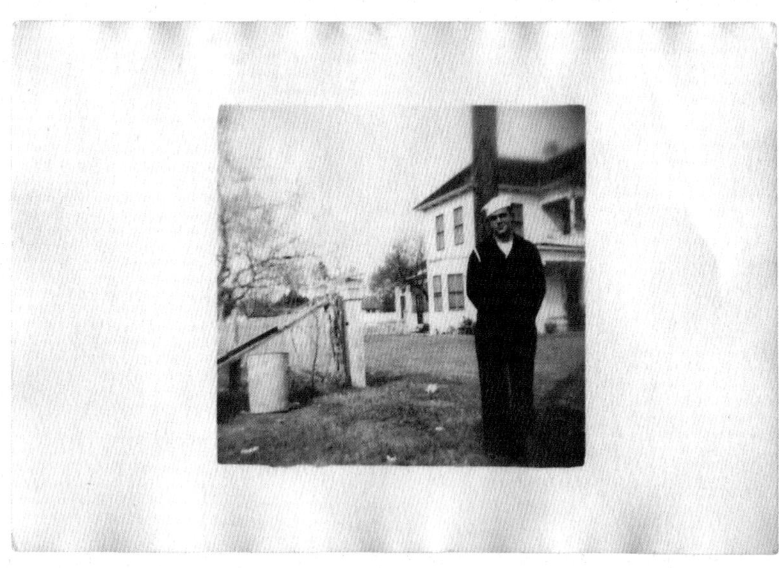

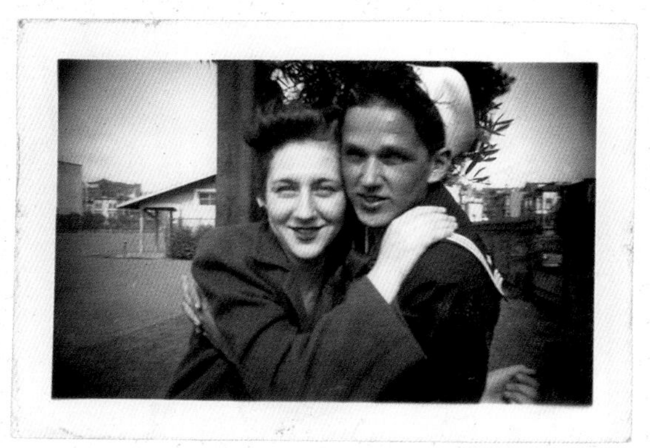

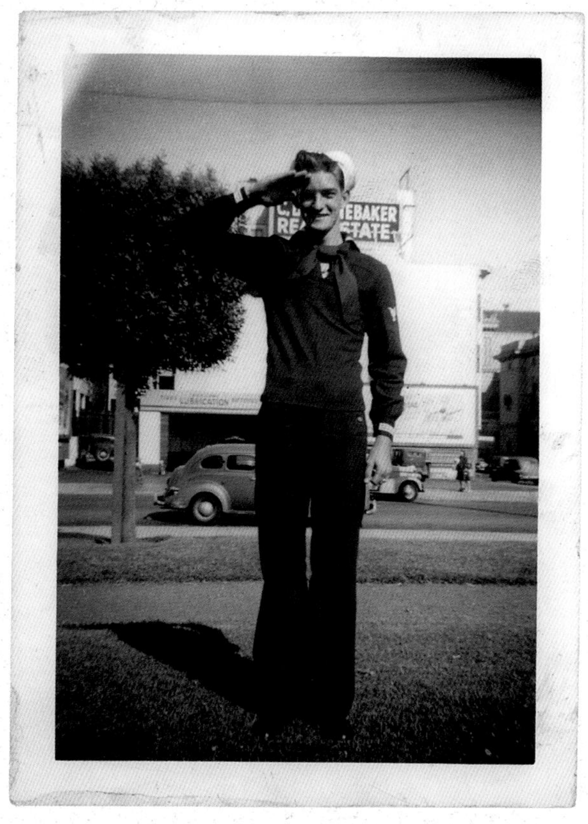
EBAKER
STATE

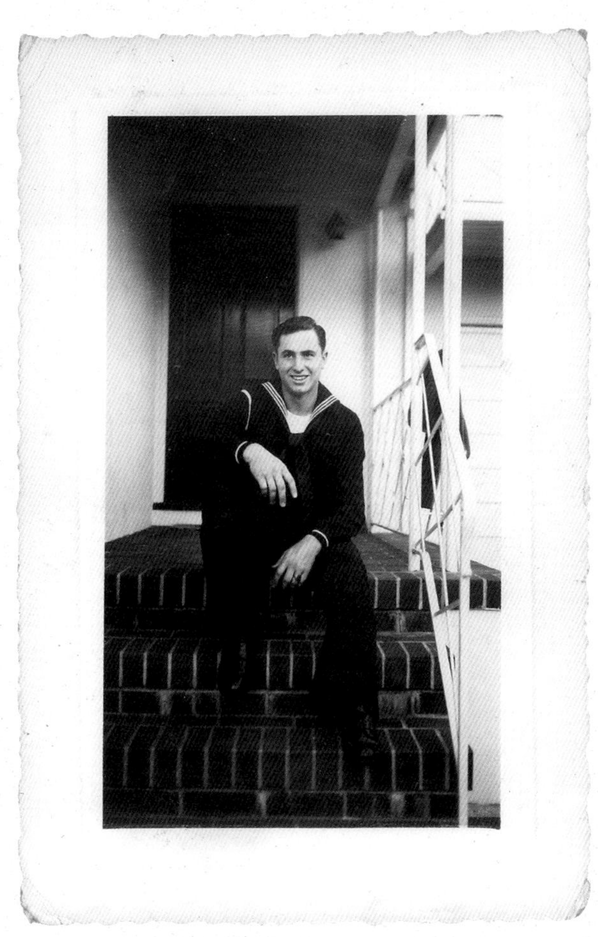

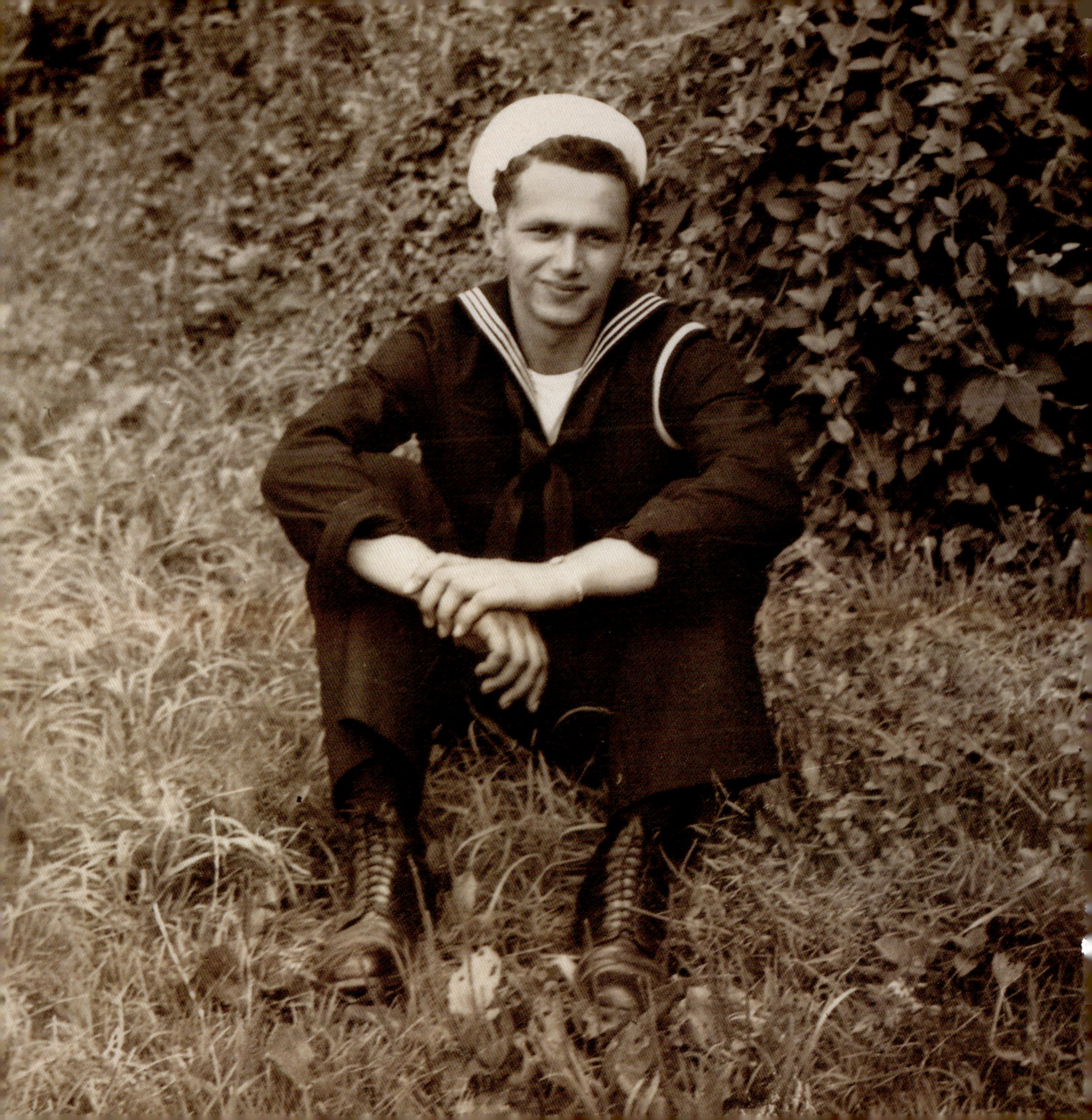

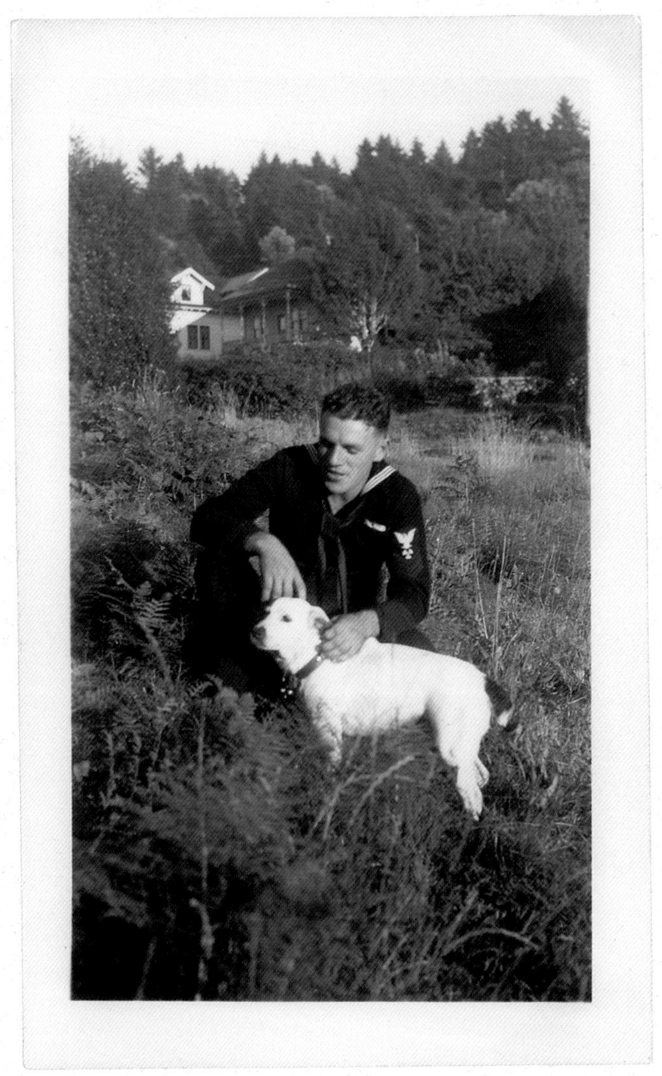

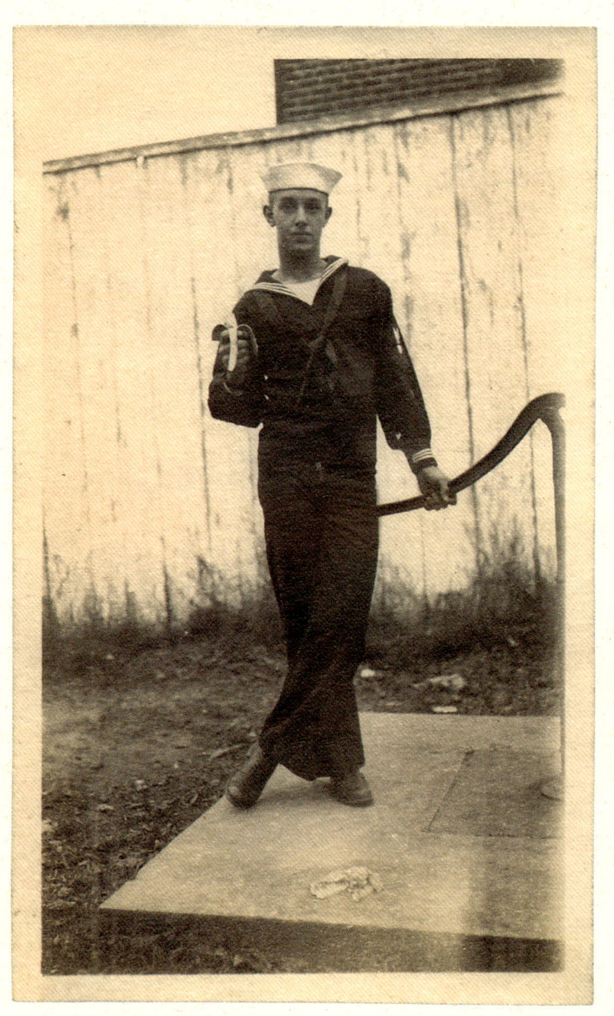

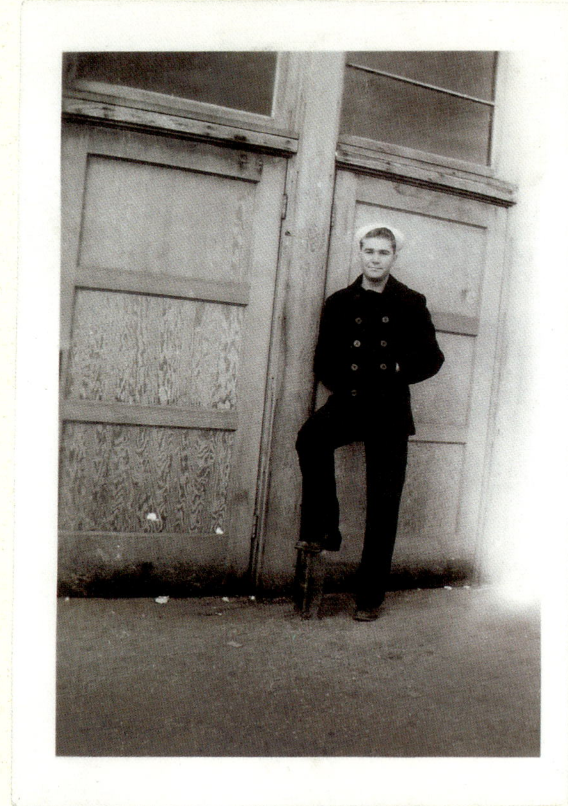

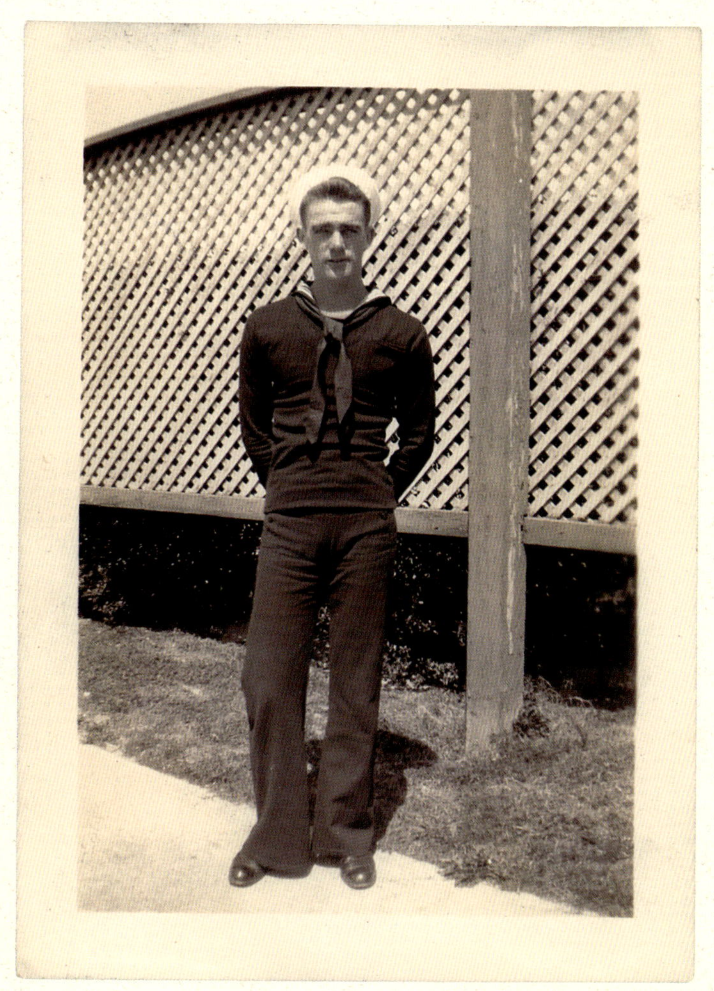

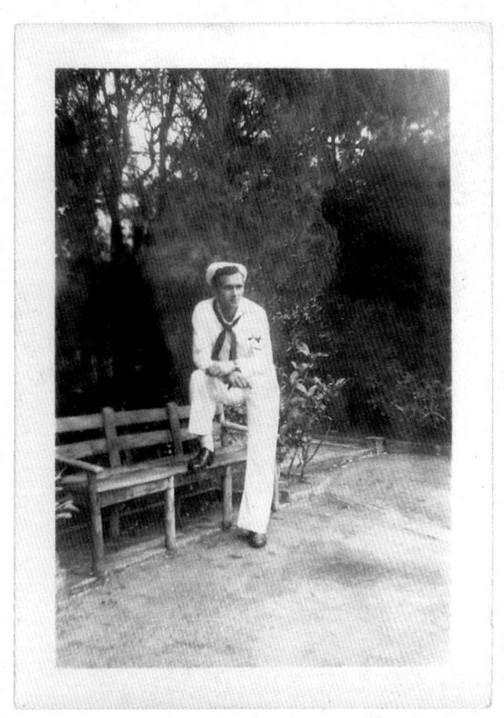

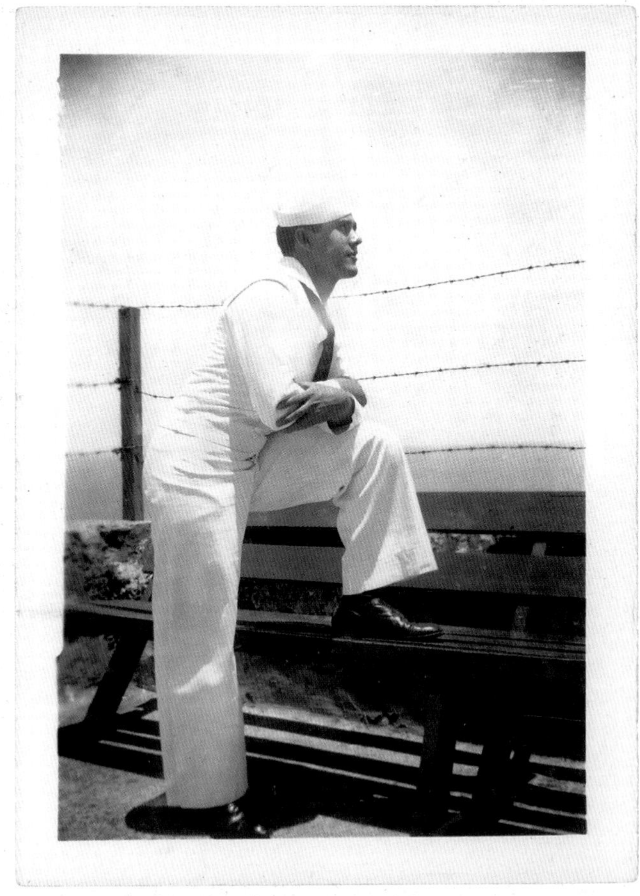

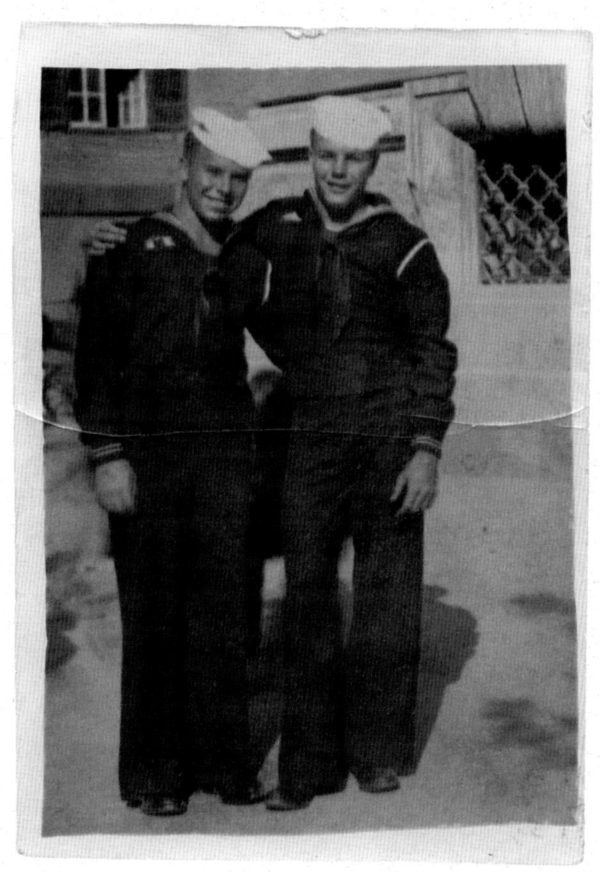

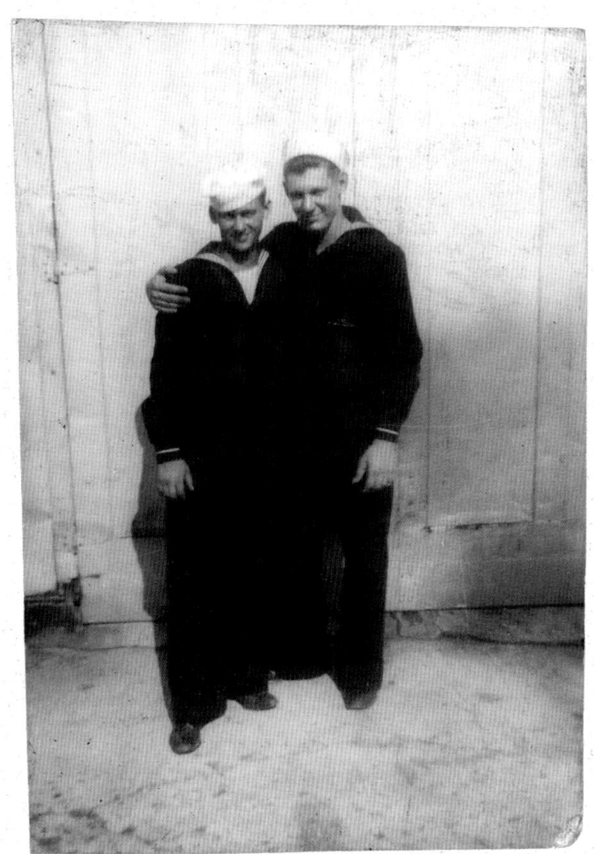

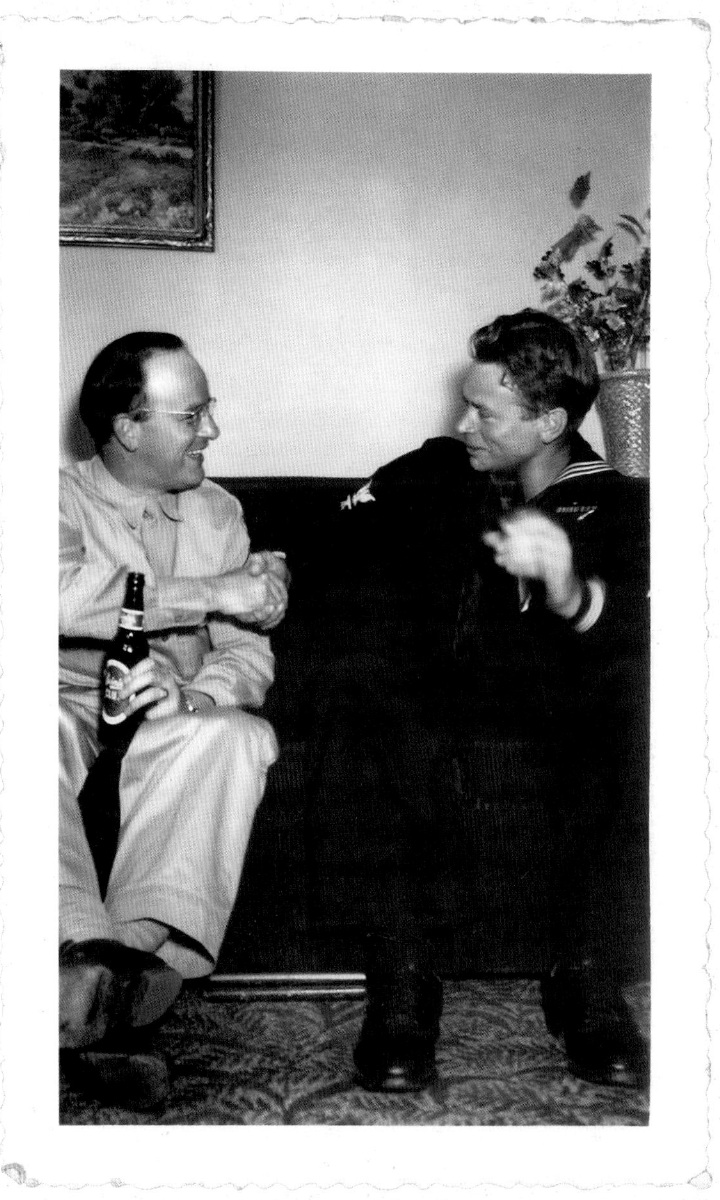

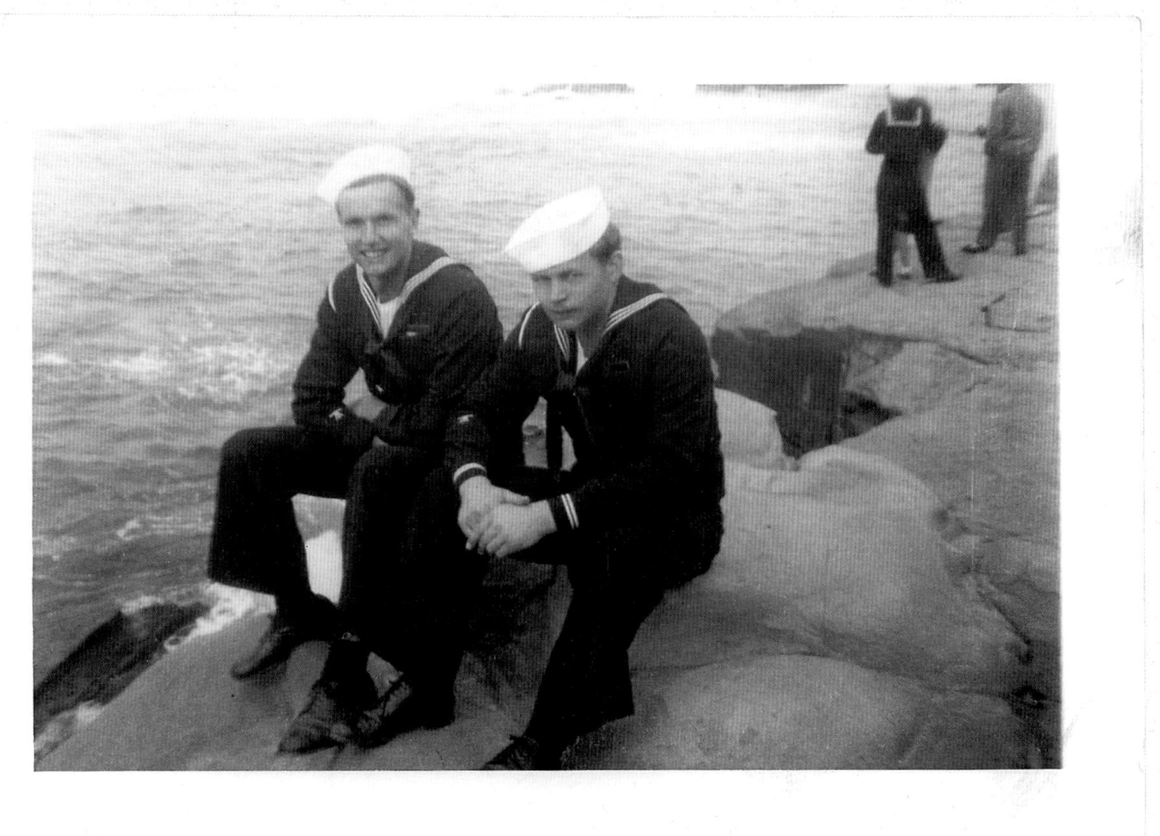

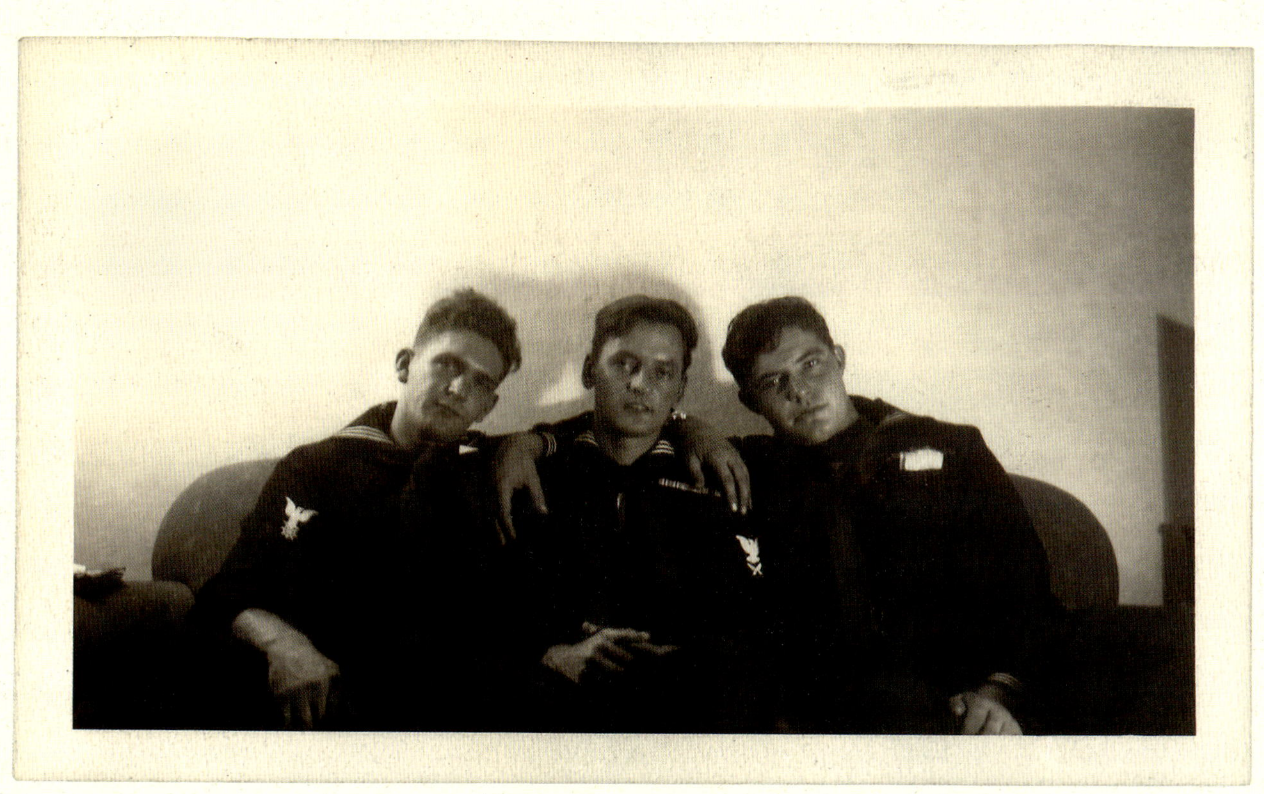

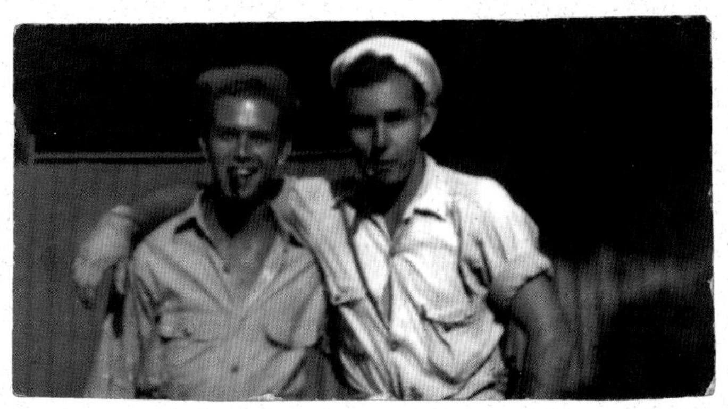

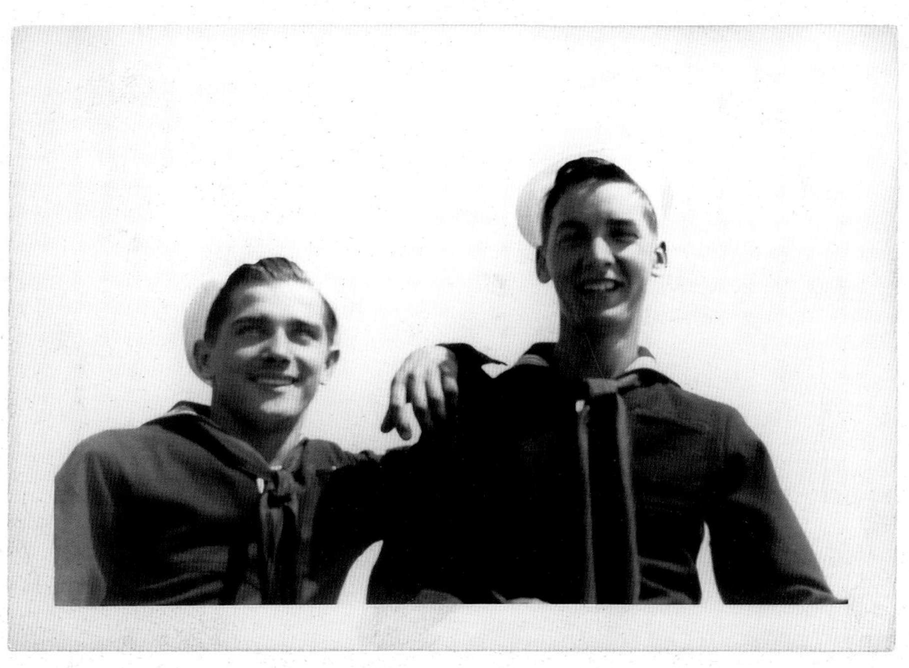

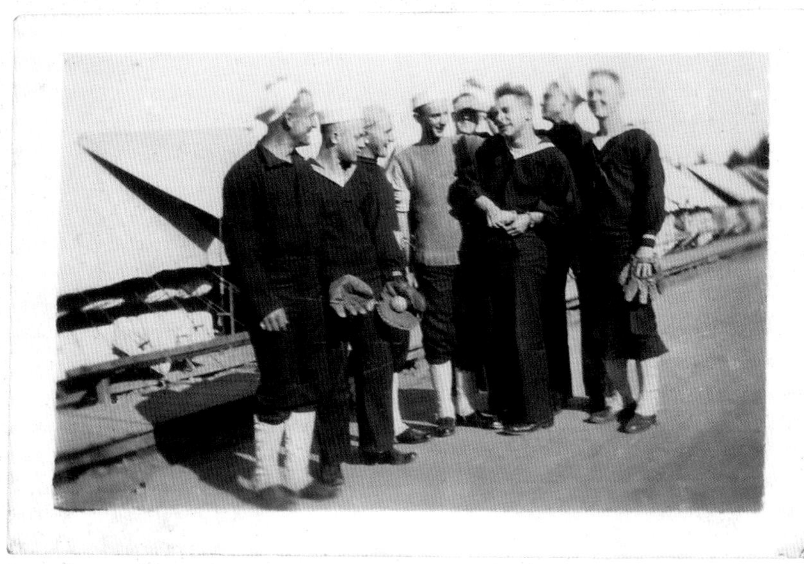

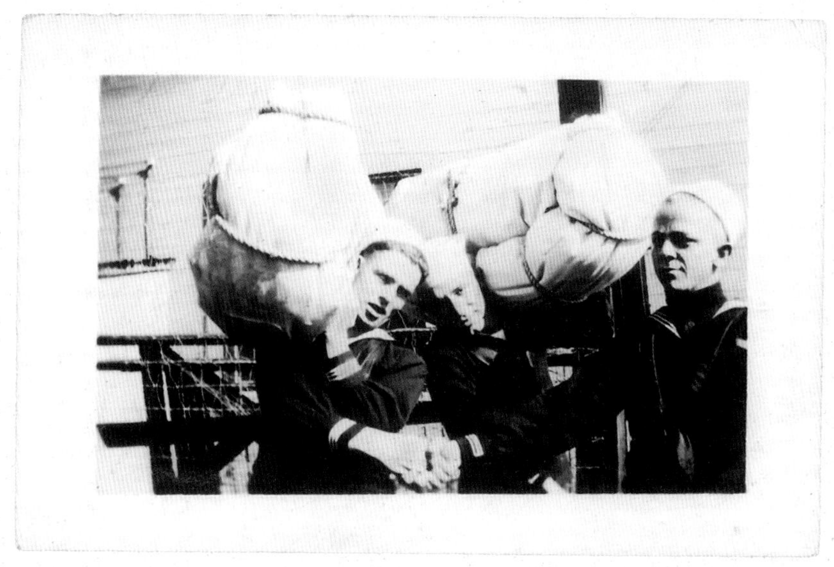

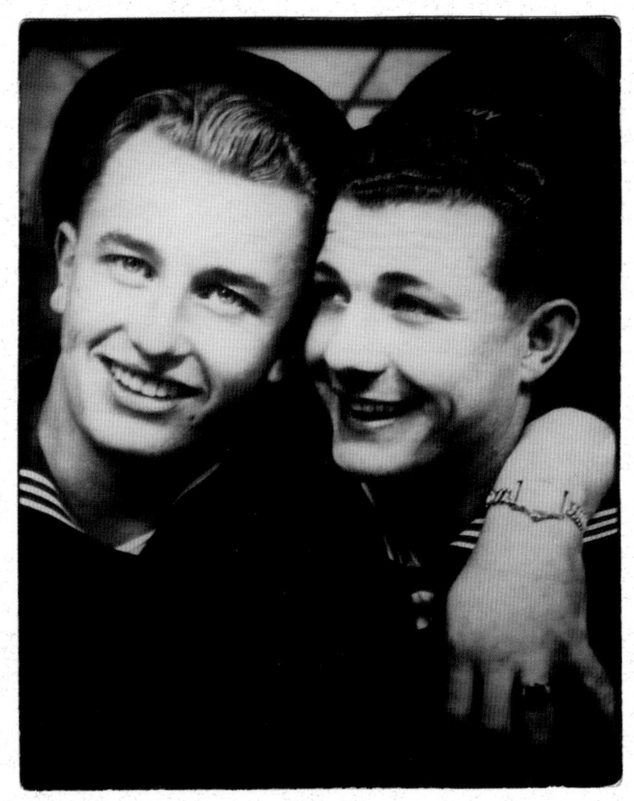

Acknowledgments

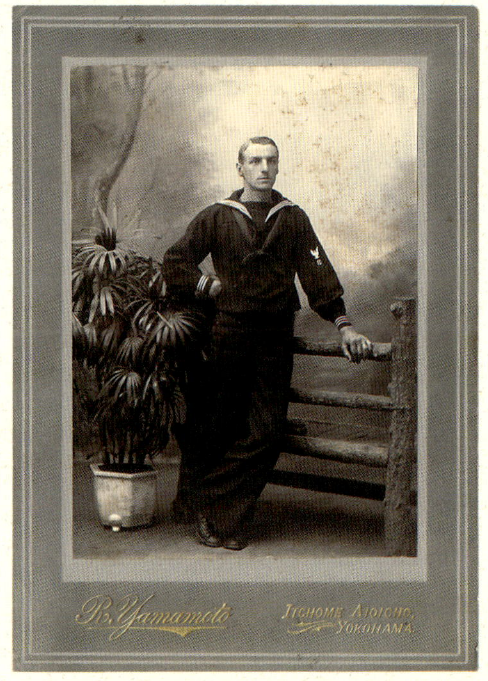

Thanks to Robert Mainardi and Trent Dunphy of The Magazine Archives, passionate collectors and preservationists, for generously allowing me to more than supplement my own photos with many wonderful images from their vast collection, and for their valuable advice and input. Thanks also to designer J. White for his dedicated partnership in this project, and for applying his discerning eye to maintaining the images as artifacts and presenting them in as visually stunning a manner as possible.

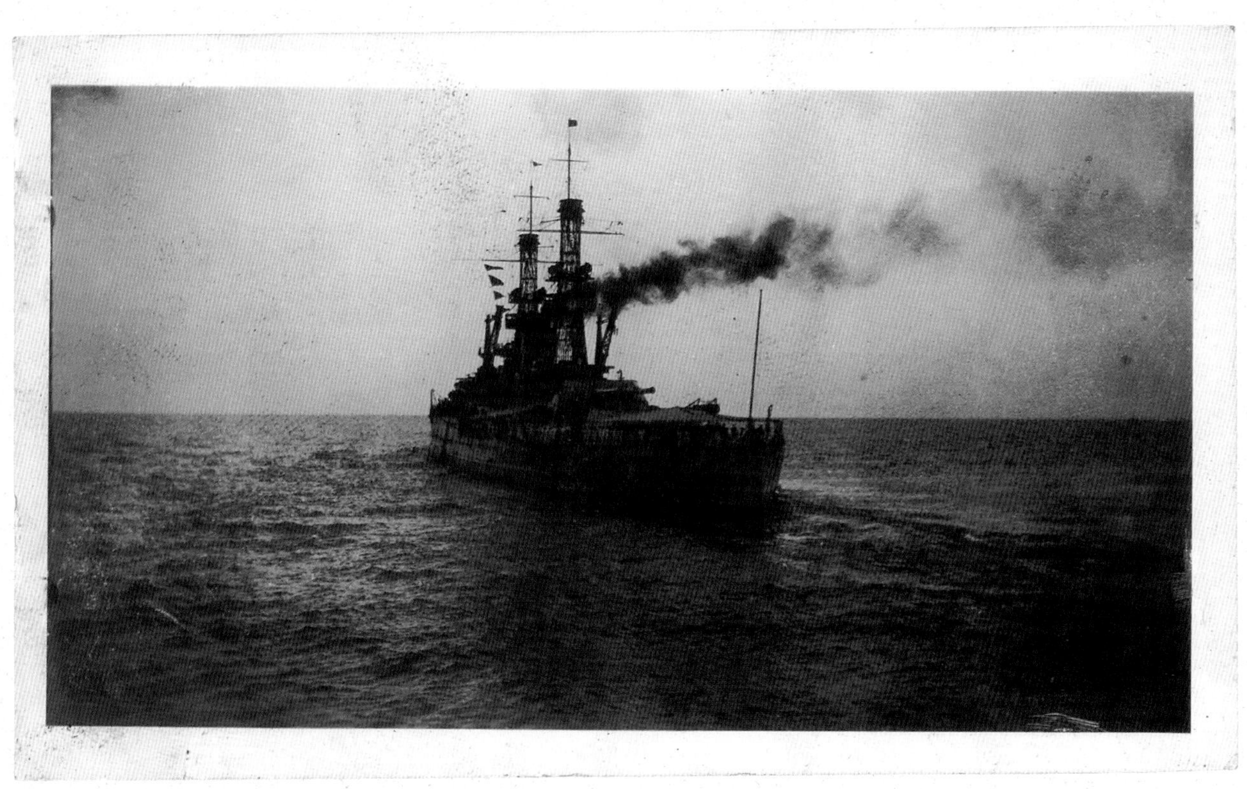

The Images

Other than the old studio names printed on the cabinet cards and a couple of portraits, all of the photographs in this book are by anonymous photographers, and are drawn from the collections of the author and The Magazine Archives. Only those photos where dates or descriptions are written on the back of the original, or where the type of image might not be apparent from its appearance on the page, are annotated here. Images listed below are snapshots unless otherwise stated. Realphoto postcards are noted as (P); cabinet cards (CC), *carte-de-visite* (CDV) and professional studio portraits should be identifiable as such on the page and are likewise only noted here if other information is given on the reverse. Images identified as *USSM* are taken from the sailor album mentioned in the introduction, chronicling a cruise aboard the *USS Maryland* in May-June 1925.

Endpapers: *Ashore in Colon, CZ,* 1925; Page ii: P, WW I; 10: CC, *Roy in Hong Kong during Spanish War;* 11: CC, *Charlie Olsen, Livermore;* 12 left: SP; right: P; 13: P, *Two old salts of the sea;* 14: *USSM;* 15: *Well what do you think of the gang. Do I look sun kissed.* c. 1920; 18 right and left: P; 21: mounted group portrait; 23: P; 27: *USSM;* 30: P; 32, 33, 36, 37 bottom: *USSM;* 37 top: P; 38, 39: *USSM;* 41: contact strips, *1945 on Minesweeper Cavalier;* 42 top: *USSM;* bottom: Dominican Republic, c. 1918; 43: *USSM;* 46: *winner in action/ pie-eating contest, October 1945;* 47 bottom, 48, 49: *USSM;* 50: photo-booth, 1925; 51: daguerreotype, c. 1850; 52 left: P; right:

tintype; 56 left: ferrotype, *G. W. May & Co., Philadelphia,* c. 1860; right: ferrotype, *W. S. Butler, Springfield, Mass.,* c. 1860; 57 right: CC, *USS St. Louis, With fondest love to Cousin Nellie from Samuel;* 58: P; 60: P, *On police duty, Oct. '23;* 61: photo-booth; 62: *Radio Gang 30 Dec 44;* 63, 64, 65 right, 66, 67: c. 1918; 68: P, c. 1910, *USS Conn/ This is a picture taken while down in Guantánamo Bay Cuba. But to see us in this picture you wouldn't think it was about the middle of March.;* 69: P; 70: *Intocicated party. Panama City;* 71: bottom, c. 1918; 73: P; 74 left: *Atop San Cristobal, San Juan, P.R. 28 July 44;* 75: China, nd; 78 left: *Dec. 9, 1945/ Golden Gate Park*; right: Mount Tamalpais, CA, c. 1920; 80 bottom: *Pepsicola for Service Men in New York;* 83 top left: *Oct '44;* bottom: *10/29/44;* 84 left: *Love to Shirly, Having a hell of a good time;* 86: P, c. 1925; 87: P; 88 right: *Was taken the 14th of Feb. in Chicago, Ill. Boy it was colder than heck that day;* 90 left: *April 15 1944;* 91 right: *JUL 6 1940;* 94: *July, 1944 San Juan, P.R.;* 98 left: *Park in San Juan, P.R. 28 July 44;* right: *"The Dreamer" or "Looking for Home" San Juan, P.R. April 29, 1944;* 102: *in my front room 11-28-45;*104 top and bottom: c. 1918; 107: USSM; copyright page: P, valentine, 1912.

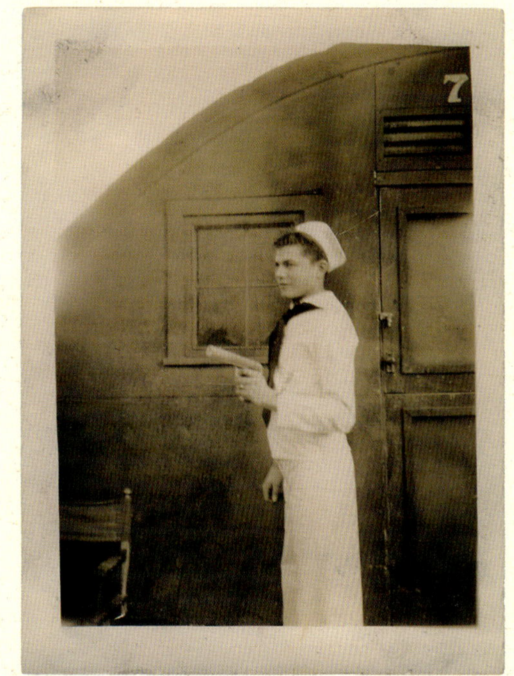

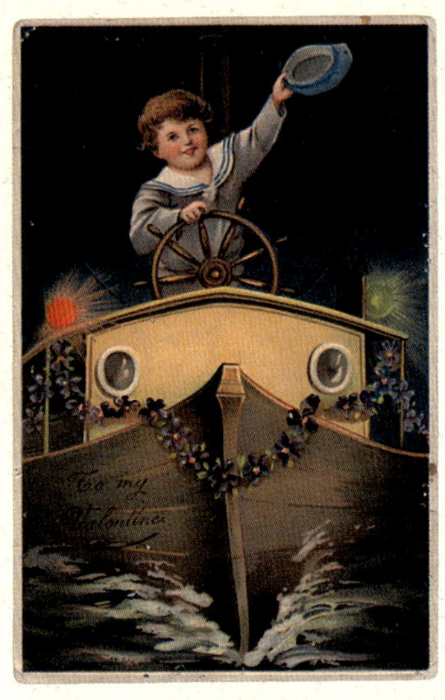

For Paul

Council Oak Books, LLC

1290 Chestnut Street, Ste. 2, San Francisco, CA 94109

1350 E. 15th Street, Tulsa, OK 74120

SAILOR: *Vintage Photos of a Masculine Icon.*

Book and jacket design by J. White.

ISBN 1-57178-094-7

First Edition / First Printing.

Printed in South Korea.

00 01 02 03 04 05 06 5 4 3 2 1

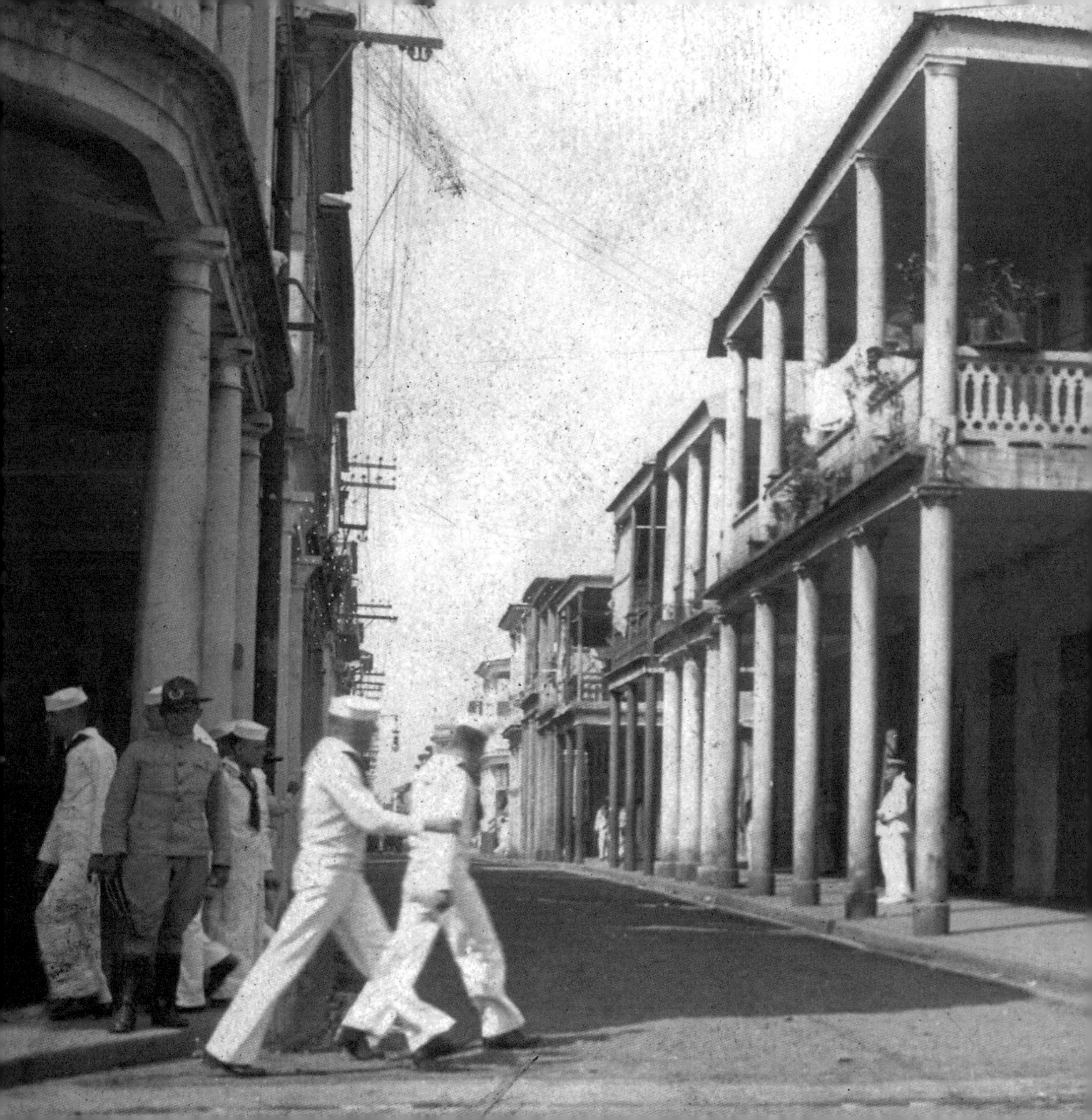